Methods of Research in Law

SECOND EDITION

DR CHARLES CHATTERJEE,
LLM (CAMBRIDGE), LLM, PhD (LONDON),
BARRISTER

OLD BAILEY PRESS

OLD BAILEY PRESS
200 Greyhound Road, London W14 9RY

First published 1997
Second edition 2000

ISBN 1 85836 386 1

British Library Cataloguing-in-Publication.

A CIP Catalogue record for this book is available from the British
Library.

Printed and bound in Great Britain.

Contents

Introduction

The term 'research' has a specific meaning. It is an investigative process whereby new facts are discovered and new concepts developed. This process admits of a method. Depending upon the nature of the discipline, the method of research may vary. However, there are always certain common elements in the methods, whether the subject be Economics, Business Studies, International Relations or Law. It would be appropriate to maintain that within the broad field of social sciences it is possible to establish a general method of doing research, although by virtue of its uniqueness each subject may require a distinctive emphasis. In this work an attempt is made to explain the basic method of doing research in law.

Research must be innovative, if not inventive. The difficulty of achieving inventive research in a non-science discipline should be appreciated. The distinction between case studies and fundamental research must be maintained. A fundamental research is primarily concerned with developing concepts upon justification.

Even though a researcher may have sufficient knowledge on the subject matter of his research, lack of training as to the method of research and techniques for analysing facts and data, where necessary, may prevent the effective utilisation of his knowledge. No work on research methodology can be exhaustive. The present work attempts to familiarise a researcher with the basic method of doing research in Law, although other researchers may find many aspects of it useful. In order to maintain a consistent style, full stops have been avoided in footnotes after 'p' or 'pp' and in citing abbreviated versions of law reports. However, given the stylistic convention of including full stops in the presentation of research papers, exceptions have been made in Chapter 8 and the Bibliography in order to illustrate this point.

Finally, throughout the work the terms 'researcher' and 'he' must be read as referring to the female gender too.

1 Ethics in Research

1.1 Introduction

This chapter deals with the standards a researcher is required to maintain in pursuing his research. It is undeniable that some research reflects a degree of dishonesty in the form of unacknowledged reference to published works, or by not being sufficiently unbiased or by not seeking what is known as 'informed consent' from the subjects. It is to be appreciated that the more ethical a researcher is in pursuing his research, the more acceptable his research is likely to be. Of course, no absolute standards may be laid down as to how to remain ethical – it primarily depends on the researcher himself. However, a few guidelines of a general nature may be offered to the researcher.

1.2 What is ethics in research?

Ethics in this context stands for '… the moral principles by which a person is guided.'[1] It would also imply that in pursuing his research he must not attempt to gain any conclusions by immoral means or that his conclusions shall not encourage immoral doings. For example, a researcher should not embark upon a research as to how to succeed in bank robberies; instead, it would be useful research if he could offer some guidelines as to how bank robberies may be prevented.

A researcher may, however, encounter an ethical dilemma in carrying out research on certain topics. In order to find the 'cause' of an 'effect' he may be required to inflict the effect on his subjects, which may be construed as unethical; but without such experiments, the cause may not be determined. Such is the case with experiments in medical science.[2] For example, human reproduction by artificial insemination should certainly be regarded as an advancement of science, but whether 'surrogacy' can satisfy all the attendant ethical questions remains controversial. The controversy surrounding the right to euthanasia represents a dilemma between Law and ethics. There are circumstances in which a doctor or a scientist may feel justified in violating ethical principles[3] or principles of human rights. A lawyer can encounter similar dilemmas too. A researcher's function should be to identify the nature of such dilemmas, and weigh the merits and disadvantages of following each of the alternatives, being mindful of his social responsibilities.

1.3 Avoidance of bias

The term 'bias' means, 'An inclination, leaning, tendency, a preponderating disposition towards, predilection; prejudice.'[4] All research must be as bias-free as possible. Given the nature of human beings generally, totally bias-free research may not be possible. Bias may arise from various sources: a researcher's family background, his educational background, that is, whether he himself received a bias-free education, the society in which he grew up, his peer group(s). These often culminate in pre-conceived ideas. A researcher must not make value judgments which are prompted by bias towards or against something. Bias may enter in the following ways:

a) pursuance of particular ideas based on the study of specific type(s) of works, published or unpublished; or
b) by choosing a specific type of subject being aware of the fact that the researcher's ideas will thereby be confirmed.

In addition to paying particular attention to the researcher's own background, attempts may be made to avoid bias in certain ways:

a) choice of topics;
b) selection of subjects;
c) selection of documents or materials;
d) determination of samples; and
e) selection of cases decided by courts and/or tribunals.

Research promoting the beliefs and convictions of a particular school of thought and avoiding examination of the rationale of other available opinions on related topics or issues, may not be regarded as bias-free research.

Avoidance of bias in legal research is of particular importance, and it is a responsibility which a researcher should take seriously. The consequences of biased research are obvious: lack of credibility and lack of validity of the research.

1.4 Some general conditions of maintaining ethics in research

Honesty with himself is the best policy in carrying out research by a researcher. He has two very important responsibilities: (a) that he has not deliberately misinformed the reader, and (b) that he has not collected information for his research by illicit or dishonest means.

This second responsibility requires a researcher to inform his subjects of the purpose(s) of collecting information from them, where necessary, and to ensure that the subjects, after being informed of the purposes, voluntarily give their consent to supply information. This process of collecting information is known as the process of 'informed consent'. Furthermore, in collecting information, a researcher must not jeopardise the self-respect and privacy of his subjects. In collecting information, for example, from prisoners, he must not give any impression of undermining them as individuals, just as he must not collect information in a way which would encroach upon the privacy of his subjects. In the end, no research should be based on information which may not be made public. A researcher must avoid causing harm to his subjects.[5] In the United States there exists a practice whereby signatures are taken from subjects on the 'informed consent' forms, but there is no guarantee that by signing an informed consent form a subject will disclose the truth. This procedure may amount to a meaningless ritual.[6]

If, however, information on the private lives of selected subjects becomes necessary for pursuing certain ideas relevant to the research, the researcher must ensure that such information is not passed to anybody or that it is destroyed.

A researcher must demonstrate his impartiality in selecting his subjects, that is, he must not select a particular type of subjects who are either ill-informed or not informed at all, or who would not argue against his actions through loyalty to him.[7]

Other major ethical points to avoid in research are: plagiarism; fabrication of data; undue exploitation of research assistants; and exposing research participants to physical or mental stress etc. A researcher should report with complete frankness the flaws in his design of research and evaluate their effect upon his findings;[8] his conclusions should be confined to those justified by the evidence he has adduced.[9] Speculative study has a limited place in research.

It is emphasised that a researcher should be ethically as neutral as possible, value-free and objective in conducting his research. His function is to study a topic by providing honest information about it and analysis of events and ideas, and to draw conclusions on the basis of his analysis.

1.5 Professional codes of ethics

Not many countries in the world have adopted professional codes of ethics pertaining to research. It was not until 1968 that the Code of the American Association for Public Opinion Research was published. Lack of awareness of the need for such codes must have led to the paucity of efforts in this regard.

The need for professional codes of ethics for research cannot be over-emphasised. Whatever may be the topic for research, a researcher should bear in mind that his subjects are 'sovereign'; they have the right not to participate nor to disclose information of a private nature, nor even to reply to the questions put to them, although the research is often ostensibly carried out in their own interest. A degree of confidence must be developed between subjects and researchers in order for all parties to derive benefits from research. Codes of conduct might develop that confidence in the minds of the informed subjects.

It would not be appropriate to ascribe any legally binding effect to codes of conduct. The basic purpose of codes being to codify the standards of behaviour of both parties, any legally binding effect of codes might run counter to encouraging research. Additionally, standards of behaviour may vary from one discipline to another. It would be extreme to suggest that research information and data should be permitted to be obtained even by coercive means, such as issuance of subpoena, or appearance before a legal tribunal.[10] The fact remains that on the grounds of public security or public policy, governments who may be subjects of research are entitled to withhold information.

After all, the arms of the Law can always be extended and employed in any legal system in order to protect the interests of both parties.

The adoption and application of a code of conduct is conditional upon the social attitudes maintained by societies towards research and of course the facilities that may be made available by them. No one type of ethical code may be applied to all societies. Nevertheless, one of the most important objectives of a code would be to encourage subjects to participate in research and to regulate the conduct of researchers according to certain set standards.

The Code of Professional Ethics and Practises of the American Association for Public Opinion Research has been designed specifically to suit the research environment in the United States. The minimum disclosure items in the Code are quite comprehensive, and perhaps applicable to any circumstances of research.

1.6 Conclusions

It is to be emphasised that no specific standards of ethics may be laid down for research. A researcher can easily adopt a very sophisticated form of 'deception' in pursuing his research. Such an act is extremely unethical as it aims at wrongfully influencing the minds of his readers. Should a researcher find it difficult to detach himself from a particular notion or idea with which his mind has been preoccupied he should not choose to do research on that topic. A researcher's primary responsibility is to his reader. His duty is to furnish the reader with true information and to analyse it without bias. Distortion of facts or analysis of facts with an ulterior motive must be avoided.

---

[1] *The Oxford English Dictionary* (2nd edition) vol V, Oxford, Clarendon Press (1989) p422.

[2] See further Paul D Reynolds, *Ethical Dilemmas and Social Science Research: An Analysis of Moral Issues Confronting Investigators in Research Using Human Participants*, San Francisco, Jossey-Bass (1979).

[3] See further M H Walizer and P L Wienir, *Research Methods and Analysis: Searching for Relationship*, New York, Harper & Row (1978), p30.

[4] *The Oxford English Dictionary*, op cit, vol II, p166.

[5] See further J F Galliher, 'The Protection of Human Subjects: A Re-examination of the Professional Code of Ethics', *American Sociologists* (1973) 93–100 at p98.

[6] See further B Thorne, 'You still Takin' Notes? Fieldwork and Problems of Informed Consent', 27 *Social Problems* (1980) 284–297 at p285.

[7] See further H C Kelman, 'Human Use of Human Subjects: The Problem of Deception in Social Psychological Experiments', *Psychological Bulletin* (1967) 111 at p5.

[8] C W Emory, *Business Research Methods*, Homewood, Illinois, Richard D Irwin (1985) p11.

[9] Ibid.

[10] See further T R Young, 'The Politics of Sociology, Gouldner, Goffman and Garfinkel', *American Sociologist* (1971) 276–281.

2 Certain Important Terms and Concepts

2.1 Introduction

The meaning of research and its objectives must be clearly understood. This chapter introduces certain terms and concepts related to research and identifies its primary objectives. Research teaches us how to discover new facts or relationships by scientific study of a subject following certain methods. On the basis of the new facts or relationships established, certain observations may be made. The collation of established ideas or published research is not true research because it lacks any originality of ideas. Familiarity with the basic methods of doing research should help establish originality of ideas; hence a knowledge of research methods is of paramount importance.

2.2 Certain important terms and concepts

Research

According to the *Oxford English Dictionary*, the term 'research' means:

'The act of searching (closely or carefully) for or after a specified thing or person.'

It also means:

'A search or investigation directed to the discovery of some fact by careful consideration or study of a subject; a course of critical or scientific inquiry.'[1]

The term 'inquiry' means investigation, which entails a method. A method is a special form of procedure, especially in any branch of mental activity, where it requires an orderly arrangement of ideas. Therefore research is a generation of new ideas by scientific study of a subject through a special form of procedure. An orderly arrangement of ideas is essential for research in any field of study.

Hypothesis

Hypothesis means: foundation, base; hence basis of an argument, supposition. According to the *Oxford English Dictionary*, 'hypothesis' means:

5

'A supposition or conjecture put forth to account for known facts; especially in the Sciences, a provisional supposition from which to draw conclusions that shall be in accordance with known facts, and which serves as a starting point for further investigation by which it may be proved or disproved, and the true theory arrived at.'[2]

A hypothesis is a vehicle for research. The basis for laying a hypothesis is the general logic pertaining to the subject-matter of research. Depending upon the nature of the topic, hypotheses will vary. If a researcher, for example, is required to do research on how football hooliganism may be dealt with, he should lay a hypothesis on the basis of his knowledge of factors associated with the general incidence of hooliganism, namely, lack of opportunity to express one's energy, broken home, lack of discipline, unemployment etc. Then, of course, gradually, he may be able to identify specific causes of hooliganism associated with the football game.

The function of laying a hypothesis is to proceed with research on the basis of certain assumptions, and through the medium of research, these assumptions may either be confirmed or rejected.

Analysis

To analyse means:

'To take to pieces; to separate, distinguish or ascertain the elements of anything complex.'
'To examine minutely, so as to determine the essential constitution, nature or form, apart from extraneous accidental surroundings.'[3]

Analysis therefore entails a minute examination of the subject-matter of a research, resolving it into simple elements. Analysis should not result in complexity. A detailed analysis requires an analytical mind with a command of the language in which the research is to be carried out and, secondly, the information required for such analysis. The nature of the topic of research will determine the components of an analysis. The purpose of the research determines the scope and type(s) of analysis required. Analysis is usually done by certain standard means: (a) selection of a sample; (b) categorisation of information; and (c) by comparison. The analysis of information will depend on the nature of the subject-matter of research.

Causation

'Causation' means 'the action of causing; production of an effect.'[4] Every effect must be preceded by a cause. It is not strictly a legal concept; it applies to a relationship between empirical events. Often it may be difficult to prove the existence of causality. In other words, a relationship between two or more variables is not necessarily a causal one;[5] the relationship may be at most partially causal. For example, if we say that 'over-eating' makes people fat, then 'over-eating' becomes the cause of making people fat. But there are many people who are fat even though they do not eat much. Again, not all causes may be direct or proximate causes. For example, if a ship sinks during the onslaught of a cyclone, one cannot say that the cyclone is the necessary proximate cause of the sinking of the ship; perhaps the ship was unseaworthy, and in that event, unseaworthiness will be the proximate cause; the cyclone should be regarded as only a remote or subsidiary cause. Again, it may not be correct to maintain that order is necessarily the effect of Law, because despite the existence of Law in many areas, there may not be any order.

Despite such difficulties in the 'causation' theory, researchers still search for causal relationships between two or more variables, and indeed, the concept of causation is not to be disregarded by them. Theoretically, the concept of causation is valid if the relationship between two or more variables is asymmetrical, that is, if a change in X results in a change in Y but not vice versa. Most importantly, the concept of causation implies that the cause must be the necessary cause, not merely a sufficient cause, to produce a result. As subjects of research multiply (individuals, consumers, States, governments etc) there may exist an indefinite number of causes. Where a causal relationship may not be established by means of scientific experiment, research hypotheses may have to be based on 'probability' or 'higher likelihood'.

Where multifarious causes and effect occur, and where a chain relationship exists between the causes, one cannot be certain as to whether any particular cause is responsible for an effect. Some authors have described this situation as one of reciprocal causation.[6]

If a researcher is satisfied that there does not exist or that there cannot be any other plausible explanation than causation, then his findings may be confirmed. Scientists aim at such conclusion. The question remains whether a researcher in Law and Social Sciences generally can reach such a conclusion. However, in the event of no alternative plausible explanation being found, the relationship between variables may be accepted as a 'causal' one.

Walizer and Wienir seem to think that 'belief in a true link' may be sufficient in confirming a causal relationship. According to them, decisions about causation must fit in with our conceptions of reality. A cause and effect assertion may not be accepted if it goes against the way we see the world.[7] However, even in that situation it must be accepted that not everybody sees the world in the same way; therefore, a researcher's different way of looking at an event or cause should not deter him from pursuing his research with a view to establishing a new concept.

Questions

A researcher may be concerned with various types of questions: open-ended questions; closed-ended questions; emotionally-loaded questions and embarrassing questions.

Open-ended questions
Open-ended questions are those questions to which there are no precise answers. For example, what is your opinion of how the government is dealing with the nuclear crisis? If a researcher offers three probable answers: very well, moderately well and badly – then this series of answers may not be of any fundamental use to him because these questions may have been addressed to those who are not informed of the complex political and defence issues attached to the nuclear crisis; secondly, no government would disclose all of the relevant information. If the researcher himself drafts the probable answers in respect of

such an open-ended question, then in this exercise he would only be able to re-affirm his conviction based on irrational answers.

Closed-ended questions

In answering closed-ended questions the respondent selects one or more of the specific categories provided by the researcher. Closed-ended questions are also known as fixed-alternative questions. The following are the main advantages of closed-ended questions:

a) respondents are required to respond in a given manner and therefore the researcher does not receive vague answers;

b) respondents may be more willing to answer closed-ended questions relating to personal affairs than open-ended questions;

c) respondents may be more willing to answer closed-ended questions because their answers are already specified and they are not required to work out their answers;

d) the probable answers being already specified, they are much easier to code or analyse; and

e) the answers being standard answers, the researcher is able to determine why certain respondents have answered his questions in a particular manner.

The following are the main disadvantages of closed-ended questions:

a) respondents are invited to answer questions in a given manner, without being given an opportunity to question the validity of those answers;

b) in the absence of an appropriate answer, respondents are still compelled to respond to a question; therefore not all answers to closed-ended questions may be honest or valid;

c) there is hardly any means of verifying whether the respondent really understood the questions or whether he misinterpreted the questions;

d) with closed-ended questions, the researcher may ignore those answers which do not fall under the chosen categories of answers; and

e) a margin of error must be allowed in that respondents may mistakenly 'tick' or 'circle' the answer(s) which they really did not wish to give.

There does not exist any conclusive answer as to whether a 'don't know' category should be included in closed-ended questionnaires. A 'don't know' category might induce a good number of respondents to shift from one of the definitive answers to the 'don't know' category. On the other hand, if the respondent really has no answer, no reliable conclusion may be drawn on the basis of a forced response.[8]

Emotionally-loaded questions

It is important that the researcher maintains his neutrality throughout his research. He must not draft questions in such a way that the answer would be affected by his emotion.

Consider, for instance, the question: since we cannot see God, would it not be better to demolish all churches, mosques, synagogues and temples? Such a proposition is bound to arouse emotion except in those who are atheists. It would be considered by the majority to be injurious to the moral fibre of a society. Even the 'don't knows' might be inclined to give their answers in the negative. Such questions may also provoke emotions in many.

Embarrassing questions

Where the subject-matter of a research relates to very personal or confidential aspects of life, it would be inappropriate to resort to surveys. In most cases the truth may not be forthcoming. However, should a researcher decide to pursue research on such subject-matter, he must assure his subjects that the confidentiality of the information they may give and their anonymity will be maintained. Despite such assurances subjects may not give the researcher true answers. As a researcher must not put to his subjects any question that may cause a degree of apprehension in the mind of the average person, he must not ask them embarrassing questions. If a researcher asks a person how many times he or she has committed adultery then probably he will not get any answer. It is a very personal question. Many may give an untrue answer to such a question. Therefore, there is no reason for raising such questions.

It must, however, be pointed out that subjects may not give any honest answers because they often feel that there is more to lose by revealing their own attitudes or deviant behaviour.[9] Questions themselves should not pose any threat to respondents or give respondents an impression of their being stigmatised.[10]

2.3 Conclusions

There is little point in discussing the concepts and terms in detail. The primary purpose of the issues raised in this chapter is to make a researcher familiar with the concept and terms related to research, so as to enable him to follow the basic rules. Legal research being a part of the general discipline called Social Sciences, a few items, such as 'questions' in their various forms, with which sociologists and psychologists are generally concerned, have been discussed in this chapter. How these concepts and terms may be applied in practice depends upon the topic of research and the purpose of a research.

---

[1] *The Oxford English Dictionary*, op cit, vol XIII, p692.

[2] *The Oxford English Dictionary*, op cit, vol VII, p582.

[3] *The Oxford English Dictionary*, op cit, vol I, p433.

[4] *The Oxford English Dictionary*, op cit, vol II, p999.

[5] K D Bailey, *Methods of Social Research*, New York, The Free Press (1982), p48.

[6] M H Walizer and P L Weiner, *Research Methods and Analysis: Searching for Relationship*, op cit, p30.

[7] Ibid p17.

[8] See further H Schuman and S Proser, 'The Open and Closed Question', 44 *American Sociological Review* (1979), p251.

[9] K D Bailey, *Methods of Social Research*, op cit, p121.

[10] See further N N Bradman and S Sudman, *Improving Interview Methods and Questionnaire Design*, San Francisco, Jossey-Bass (1979).

3   Tools of Research

3.1 Introduction

There are certain traditional tools of research, but the extent to which they should be employed depends upon the discipline in which the research is to be carried out. Tools of research are often employed with a view to collecting information of a secondary nature. In this chapter an attempt is made to identify the tools that may generally be employed by a researcher in Law.

3.2 Meaning and use of tools of research

The term 'tools' in this context refers to the means that may be employed by a researcher in order to collect data. Primary sources of information[1] do not entail application of any tools, as they are already identifiable. It is some of the secondary sources of information[2] the collection of which requires certain tools, namely interviews, questionnaires, experience surveys, case studies, computers etc. Tools should not be confused with sources: tools are the means of exploring and exploiting probable sources of information, usually of a secondary nature. Tools are different from aids, such as dictionaries, statutes guiding interpretation of certain standard legal terms etc. The latter are primarily used by courts and tribunals for clarification of the provisions of statutes.

The tools of research are to be determined prior to developing any research, and depend upon time, availability of funds, availability of subjects and of course the nature of the topic for research.

The following represent the most popular tools of research:

a) published works (books and articles);
b) interviews;
c) questionnaires;
d) case studies;

e) experience surveys; and
f) computers.

Tools of research are means to an end; the end of legal research should be to establish fundamental ideas in a chosen area of law. A researcher in Law should take care that he does not detract from the validity and reliability of his research.

In view of their ever-increasing use in research, a separate section is provided on computers.

3.3 The use of computers in legal research

The advent of computers has certainly been beneficial for researchers. Information, including consolidated information, especially on published works in a given field of research, is now made easily accessible by computers. Computers help standardise information and, as time-saving aids, should be used by all researchers, no intensive training being necessary.

However, the caution should be entered that a researcher should not misuse or abuse computers by feeding them only with selective information. Information on computers is usually of a secondary nature – although primary data may also be made available by them. Computers mainly provide information on published books, articles, or survey reports etc, although information on decided cases is usually available on them, too. The status of computer-based information may depend upon the status of the provider of the information. For example, information provided by a government department or a police department or a reputable research institution carries authority. Computers are certainly very helpful for researchers in Law, particularly in the initial information-gathering period of research.

The interaction and the benefits of the Internet are gradually changing the way in which legal work and research have been carried out for decades. If the computers are seen as the technical libraries of information, the Internet is the transmitter of that information in a simple and inexpensive way.

Since the early 80's lawyers have turned to computers to store their extensive paper information. At the inception of the Internet many saw the possibilities of using this stored information in legal research but the fear of something new, the paucity and slowness of access, high cost and the huge gaps in its content deterred them from such a resource.

However, remarkable changes have taken place over a very short period and millions of people are now using the Internet every day to communicate, learn and carry out research. It is certainly an ingenious tool for those involved in legal work of all kinds. One does not even have to be a computer expert or a technical genius to access this service. All that is needed is a PC, a modem, a Web browser and an Internet Account.

There are several sites on the World Wide Web (www) that maintain virtual law libraries as well as reference sources for their targeted audience. The most useful legal sites in the UK are as follows.

• Parliamentary site
• Government Information Service

- The Lawyer
- The Times (on-line registration required)
- Lord Chancellor's Department
- Lawlinks
- DTI
- The Court Service

LEXIS and Lawtel Europa have been the leading providers of online legal information in the UK since the early 70's and set up to help the legal practitioners research the law more efficiently. These databases include extensive coverage of case laws, articles, legislation and full text of official transcripts of EU documents. In order for users to be able to search for materials easily the material is broken down into libraries and then sub-divided into sets of files. *LEXIS* depends on full-text research and retrieval whereas Lawtel relies on summaries, which allows its system to be updated quickly. Lawtel contains a daily update section providing a brief description of all new documents added to the database in the last 24 hours which makes it more up-to-date than most electronic services.

Readers' attention is drawn to: Westlaw UK as a full text online subscription service, Butterworths Direct which as all the traditional sources such as *Halsbury's* and *All England Law Reports* online and a huge range of CD-Rom services.

Access to the legal documents is no longer restricted to *LEXIS* or Lawtel but can now be obtainable from the above sites as well as from the databases provided for free by public and private organisations and from collections created by lawyers and law libraries. One of the most unique ways to conduct research on the Internet is the ability to ask one of the search engines, which are indexes of the Web sites to scour the Web internationally and return with the information required. Resources for students to access the availability of training contracts and pupillages include the following.

- gti
- prospects legal
- student law centre
- Law Careers.net
- lawgazette.co.uk

As increasingly people are becoming involved in cross-border transactions, law firms need to ensure that they have the best advice in foreign jurisdictions. Universities similarly need to ensure that they equip the future lawyers with enough resources to be able to access such up-to-date information and interpret its application for their clients.

Here are some of the important web addresses where students can find valuable free sources of information.

www.venables.co.uk/legal/   This gives access to Government and parliamentary sites, the Law Society and information on the law firms on the internet.

www.hmso.gov.uk/stat.htm   All statutory instruments from 1 January 1997.

www.bailii.org	Collects British and Irish legislation and law reports on a single searchable site (British and Irish Legal Information Institute).
www.hmso.gov.uk/acts.htm	New statutory Acts of parliament from 1 January 1996.
www.parliament.uk	House of Commons and Lords debate.
www.studentlaw.com	Student Law Centre.
www.gti.co.uk	GTI.
www.lawgazette.co.uk	The Law Society Gazette.

All the sites and their options can be accessed through the 'venables' site.

The Law courseware package developed for students is called IOLIS. A consortium of universities created and developed this. It contains interactive workbooks on different areas of Law, all on one compact disc (CD).

Students can also access the Electronic Law Reports (ELR) package which contains the complete text of the full Law Reports Series up to 1996. Similarly other packages like Butterworths Company Law Handbook, Butterworths Company Law Service, Blackstone's Criminal Practice are all available electronically.

The next item to explore is how to access the e-mail system. E-mail is one of the easiest and most used areas of the Internet. It is fast and cheap and for many people this is the only aspect of the Internet which is extensively used.

E-mail addresses have three elements: a username, an @ sign and a domain name. The username is usually the name which is used to log on to the computer. The domain name is the address of the service provider or online service one is using. For example, if the person's username is joe.bloggs, and the service provider's address is freeserve.co.uk, then his e-mail address will be joe.bloggs@freeserve.co.uk.

To send a message one needs to create the message. In Outlook Express it is called 'Compose Message'. The features in the mail message window are the same in any programme.

To: this is where the e-mail address of the person the message is being sent to is typed in.
cc: this is the same as sending the copy of a letter to other recipients. Type in the e-mail addresses of the recipients separated by a semi-colon and a space.
bcc: this field is used when one does not want some of the recipients to know who else is receiving a copy.
From: this is where the sender's e-mail address is entered automatically.
Subject: a short description of the message should be entered in this field as the name suggests.
Attached: this is used to attach any computer files that the sender wants to send to the recipient.

Below these fields is the area for the message to be typed. The send button is usually marked in any e-mail programme. E-mail is not only used for sending and receiving mail but also for replying and forwarding incoming messages (see also Chapter 7).

3.4 Survey research

Tools of research help carry out surveys. The purpose of a fundamental research is much higher than that of a survey. A researcher should therefore ensure that the limitations of a survey are clearly stated in his research and that no fundamental conclusions are reached on the basis of survey research as such research being based on probabilities. The legal research for which such summary research may be used may not admit of sufficient degree of reliability. Results of survey research may be employed only with a view to seeking information, primarily of a secondary nature, in pursuing legal research. Survey research, on the other hand, may serve some special purpose when carrying out legal research in, for example, consumer protection or issues relating to housing or health etc.

3.5 Conclusions

It is essential that, prior to his embarking upon a research, a researcher considers the type(s) of tools to be employed. The validity of legal research very much depends upon this factor. Furthermore, the selection of topics for research also depends upon this factor. All these points are discussed in Chapters 4, 5 and 6 of this work.

In the case of research in an interdisciplinary topic embracing, for example, Law, Economics and Business Studies, resort to survey research may be necessary. A student of Law may be required to rely upon multiple methods of research as each discipline has its unique method of research. It would be appropriate for a researcher who wishes to carry out his research in a multidisciplinary topic to mention at the beginning of his dissertation/thesis the types of method he has used.

---

[1] See Chapter 5.
[2] See Chapter 6.

4 Research Planning and Research Design

4.1 Introduction

Planning a research project depends upon the nature of the subject-matter and the availability of material. Care should be taken that a research does not represent a summary of previous research in the same field of study.

Included in research planning are choice of a topic, identification of issues, formulation of questions, laying of hypotheses and research design. Of these, the choice of a topic is the most important because on this depends how the other required measures may be taken.

4.2 Factors affecting the choice of a topic

There can be a number of factors affecting the choice of a topic. Of these the most important ones are:

a) familiarity of the researcher with the topic – a general knowledge of the basic subject-matter is essential so that the researcher may identify the more complex issues;
b) the importance of research on a topic at a particular point in time;
c) availability of materials – both primary and secondary;
d) the researcher's values[1] – his values may be created by his upbringing, his education and the influence of the society and culture in which he has been brought up;
e) his social, political and/or business paradigms, that is, the school of thought with which the researcher identifies himself – this is also interrelated with the previous item (values);
f) the nature of research – pure or applied;

g) the response a researcher might receive from his subjects; and

h) the time and finance that may be entailed in a project.

A researcher may wish to avoid a topic which is emotionally-loaded, unless of course he has been sponsored by an institution to carry out such research. In that event it must be borne in mind that his research may develop only one point of view. Research of a topic which is heavily concerned with governmental secrets or policy matters relating to State security and defence is bound to encounter difficulties. Similarly, unless legislation as to disclosure of all the business activities of business organisations makes it obligatory for them to disclose information, where necessary, a researcher may not be able to obtain honest and correct information on the business activities of a business organisation or corporate body. Research in topics which encroach upon privacy may have to be based on unrepresentative information and data.

All research should be problem-based. The investigation of a problem is not the sum of research; it must provide answers to some of the questions raised.

4.3 Identification of issues

The identification of issues is an integral and indeed paramount part of the research process. One of the most important objectives of applied research is to collect information with a view to solving a problem. A researcher should ask himself first, what he would like to achieve through his research. The clearer the goal, the clearer the question will be. He must also set his questions and if possible in a hierarchical order.

Identification of issues and resolution of problems are two different things. Not all issues may have a resolution; issues must be identified regardless of the prospect of their resolution, because without identification of issues, the choice of a problem will be a useless effort. In determining the issues, the researcher must be as honest and neutral as possible. Identification of issues is equally important for both pure research and research of an applied nature. It is sometimes difficult to maintain a watertight division between these two aspects of research. It would, therefore, be wrong to assume that questions relevant to pure research are not relevant to applied research.

4.4 Research design

According to Walizer and Wienir, the ways of collecting data are often referred to as research design.[2] But this is only one aspect of research design. Research design is concerned with the structure, plan and method(s) of investigation with a view to reaching acceptable answers to research questions.

Phillips maintains that the research design constitutes the blueprint for the collection, measurement and analysis of data.[3] A research design serves two purposes: (a) it helps the researcher to make a rational allocation of his resources for collecting material for his research; and (b) it allows him to identify the tools he may require for his research.

It could be said that research design stands for a plan to attain the objectives of research through certain methods such as utilisation of appropriate sources, collection of data, testing and evaluation of hypotheses and conclusions.

4.5 How to develop a formal research design

The development of a formal research design largely depends upon the nature of the specific project. It is, however, possible to offer general guidelines as to how to develop a research design, as all research in Law shares certain common elements of procedure.

a) The major concepts must be defined – at this stage, the secondary concepts that may emerge must also be defined.
b) The primary and secondary issues must be identified.
c) The tools of research must be determined – surveys, interviews, whether informally or through questionnaires, mailed or otherwise, and collection of data, where appropriate.
d) The shortcomings or limitations of the research must be clearly stated.

It is to be borne in mind, however, that a workable research design may be prepared only if the researcher is familiar with the basic problems, issues and published works relating to the topic of his research.

4.6 Exploration of problems

Exploration of problems is necessary because it saves time and expense. It would also reduce the chances of designing a research on the wrong basis. The primary methods of exploration are literature search and experience survey.

The purpose of literature search is not to look for new ideas but to find out what has already been explored in a related area and under what conditions. The objectives of research will be defeated if the researcher totally relies on the assumptions and conclusions made by previous researchers. Literature search provides a background to the area of interest.

Experience survey is less precise than literature search. It consists of seeking information from persons experienced in the area of research. War veterans, people engaged in relief work or prison officers, for example, can provide valuable practical information in their respective areas. In the case of experience survey, it is for the researcher to categorise information according to his requirements. In this type of survey not only the opinions of veterans but also the opinions of newcomers or critics can be very useful.

Exploration is discovery. It is for the researcher to explain what he has explored. The purpose of the exercise is not merely to gather information but also to acquire insight into a matter.[4]

4.7 Conflicts in designing a research

Conflicts in research design may arise from various sources:

a) the researcher's own perception of problems and ideas pertaining to the topic;
b) the problem as it is seen by clients;
c) how the business organisations involved in the area of research perceive the problems; and
d) the views held by various action groups.

This can be illustrated by means of an example – conflict of interests between the parties in relation to private foreign investment. Clients in this context are host countries. They would like to see that private foreign investment contributes to their economy and that their resources, including natural and human, are utilised according to their plans and predetermined priorities. Additionally, in order to ensure that private foreign investors do not dominate their economy, host countries would also like to participate in the management and administration of foreign investments. Furthermore, development should not be achieved at the cost of cultural values. In other words, host countries would like to attain economic diversity without unduly disturbing their cultural values.

Private foreign investors, on the other hand, are in the final analysis profit-making enterprises. Their priorities are very different from those of the host countries. Their own available expertise would normally prompt them to determine their priorities of investment. The enterprises would also like to ensure their control over their investment abroad – that is, as much participation as possible in investments. Finally, included in their aims are repatriation of profits, non-disclosure of techniques of production/manufacture unless made obligatory by a host country, and sales of those products and services over which they enjoy expertise.

Realising the nature of these conflicts between private foreign investors and developing countries, in particular, various institutions have developed codes of conduct with a view to regulating the conduct of such investors.[5] Care should be taken that the researcher remains neutral and is not influenced by the perceptions either of home countries or of host countries.

In designing his research a researcher should bring out these conflicts, their origins and the nature of continuing conflicts etc. Additionally, the views given by various institutions engaged in resolving these conflicts, in developed and developing countries, in addition to those advanced by various international, inter-governmental and non-governmental organisations, should be critically examined. It would also be important to study the position of both sets of countries, developed and developing, as home and host countries. Finally, in designing research on this topic, it is essential to explore the purposes of various developed and developing countries in accepting private foreign investments. It would also be appropriate to consider various dimensions of development as perceived by both developed and developing countries.

4.8 Conclusions

Research planning and design is a complex process. There is no standard formula as to how to plan and design a research. It depends upon various factors: whether the study is observational or exploratory, a mere statistical study or experimental, or pure research. One of the most important factors in planning and designing a research is the availability of information; therefore, a preliminary survey of the possible sources of information is advisable. Time-scale is also an important factor in this regard. A research design should pass through two stages: first, an exploratory stage which helps lay hypotheses; and second, the specific research. A research design identifies the strategies through which a plan of research is to be carried out. This is the basis for interdependence between a research plan and a research design. Depending upon the nature of the topic and the purposes of research, both plan and design will have to be made.[6]

---

[1] According to Bailey, '… values affect not only the problem deemed worthy of research but also the method considered appropriate and the way the researcher views the relationship between himself and his or her subjects.' See K D Bailey, op cit, p19.

[2] Walizer and Wienir, op cit, p231.

[3] B S Phillips, *Social Research Strategy and Tactics*, New York, Macmillan (1971), p93.

[4] C W Emory, op cit, p63.

[5] See, for example, *The Proposed Text of the Draft Code of Conduct on Transnational Corporations*, New York, UN (1988) E/1988/39/Addl.

[6] See further C W Emory, op cit, p81.

5 Sources of Information – I

5.1 Introduction

This chapter is intended to emphasise the importance of sources of information in research. It has been pointed out that in order for a research to attain credibility, it must rely upon primary sources of information rather than sources of a secondary nature. Included in this chapter is also a discussion of the merits of relying upon documents of a primary nature.

5.2 A general discussion of primary and secondary sources of information

Primary sources are those sources which are direct, authoritative and not influenced by anybody's opinion. Under this category will fall documents of an original nature or legislation or statutes or treaties or any other document of similar status. A company's articles and memorandum or its annual report is a primary source of information for that company. To satisfy the requirements of the primary source, a document must be original and it must have been prepared as of necessity. Such documents include, for example, minutes of meetings, presidential proclamations and records of proceedings, discussion in Parliament or legislature. In special circumstances, personal diaries and autobiographies may be regarded as primary sources.

Secondary sources are those sources which are not of a primary nature. Opinions of experts, books and published articles generally are examples of secondary sources of information. All such materials are called 'reference materials'. They are so called because a researcher, in support of his views or to disagree to others' views, refers to them.

Like fountains, primary sources always remain alive. The age of a primary source is of no importance. Primary sources of information are free from views or opinions; they are mere statements of facts or events. The resolutions of international, inter-governmental or non-governmental bodies, however old or recent, are primary sources. A dictionary is a primary source of information because it is regarded as the most acceptable source of the most appropriate etymological meanings of words. Commentaries on a document of a primary nature are not regarded as primary sources of information unless they have been produced or prepared by the author(s) of the original document, such as an approved commentary by a Senate Committee or the Congress in the United States or by the Parliament of a country. Speeches by heads of government of States are primary sources of information, when documented ad verbatim. Interpretations of such speeches are secondary sources of information. All religious scriptures are regarded as primary sources of information. A statute or an Act of a Parliament or a legislative body is a primary source of information, as is the authenticated version of a judgment of a court of law or award of a tribunal. A primary source of information does not admit of anybody's knowledge, experience etc.

The method of collecting information may help designate a source as primary or secondary. For example, a telephone conversation, if recorded, may in certain circumstances (perhaps between two heads of State) be regarded as a primary source of information, but not so if interpreted. Only the original of a document of a primary nature is a primary source, not its photocopy or carbon copy. Of course, authenticated texts of treaties translated into various languages are regarded as primary sources. Conflicting documents on the same subject-matter cannot be regarded as primary sources of information until the conflict as to the authenticity of one of them has been resolved. Documents written under duress are not documents representing primary sources of information, because they are not genuine documents.

5.3 Merits of studying documents of a primary nature

Primary documents represent accurate records or statements of events. Once their authenticity has been established, they cannot be disregarded. They are permanent records. Any change or even the abolition of the institution that originated the document does not diminish the authenticity of a document of a primary nature. Information based on authentic documents need not be verified. In many cases a study of the recorded discussions that led to the conclusion of a document serves a very useful purpose in determining the reason for its conclusion.

Documents in this context should be divided into two categories: public and private. Public documents are those documents which have been prepared by public authorities such as government departments, governmental institutions, international institutions, inter-governmental institutions etc. Public documents are open to members of the public, unless they are categorised by such institutions as 'confidential'. Governmental institutions can also categorise certain documents as 'confidential' documents. In that event, a researcher cannot refer to them. Any document which is not addressed to the public, nor meant for public use, cannot be relied upon for research.

Treaties, notes of exchange between governments, and parliamentary papers provide primary information on various matters. The preambles to such documents often provide good background information justifying their conclusion, and they may be used as primary sources of information. For example, the Preamble to the Treaty between the Government

21

of the United States of America and the Government of Canada on Mutual Legal Assistance in Criminal Matters of March 18, 1985 provides that:

> 'The Government of the United States of America and the Government of Canada
>   Desiring to improve the effectiveness of both countries in the investigation, prosecution and suppression of crime through cooperation and mutual assistance in law enforcement matters,
>   Have agreed as follows:' [1]

The more a researcher relies upon primary documents, the more reliable will be his results.

5.4 List of some of the important local institutions from which information may be available

A researcher is often required to collect his material and information from various libraries and institutions. Below is a list of certain of the important libraries and institutions which a researcher may find useful. This list is by no means exhaustive; quite often a local borough library may provide useful information.

- The British Library
- The Bodlein Library in Oxford
- Commonwealth Secretariat Library
- Public Records Office
- The Bank of England
- The Chartered Insurance Institute
- The Institute of Bankers
- The Department of Trade and Industry
- The Inns of Courts Libraries (open to enrolled Barristers only)
- The Law Society (open to enrolled individuals only)
- The National Consumers' Association
- The City Business Library
- The Guildhall Library
- The British Medical Association (Medicine and the Law)
- The Wellcome Foundation (Medicine and the Law)
- Chatham House (International Relations, International Law and the United Nations)

As to the European Union materials, a researcher may find the following libraries useful: the European Parliament and the European Union Office in London. As to UN materials, the United Nations Information Centre in London has a small library. A researcher carrying out research on international law-related topics may find it helpful to use the main UN Libraries in New York and Geneva, and the libraries of the Specialised Agencies of the UN concerned, which are located in various parts of the world – if, of course, the required materials are not available in his own university library. Incidentally, many of the EU and UN materials may be obtained at Her Majesty's Stationery Office (HMSO) Bookshop in London.

It must be pointed out that a researcher has no automatic right of entry into any of these libraries. Admissions are by permission of the authorities concerned and are often subject to an admission fee. Researchers should primarily depend upon their respective university law libraries, and the inter-library loan arrangements that operate between university libraries. Certain libraries may not be open to undergraduate students at all.

5.5 UN libraries

UN Headquarters (UN)
New York, NY 10017
USA

UN Office at Geneva
Palais des Nations,
8–14 Avenue de la Paix,
1211 Geneva 10,
Switzerland

UN Office at Vienna
Vienna International Centre,
PO Box 500,
A–1400 Vienna,
Austria

UN Information Centre in London
21st Floor Millbank Tower,
Millbank,
London, SW1P 4QP

Other Offices

UN Children's Fund (UNICEF)
3 United Nations Plaza,
New York, NY 10017
USA

UN Conference on Trade and Development (UNCTAD)
Palais des Nations,
1211 Geneva 10,
Switzerland

UN Population Fund
220 East 42nd Street,
New York, NY 10017–5880
USA

UN Institute for Training & Research (UNITAR)
Palais des Nations,
1211 Geneva 10,
Switzerland

UN Environment Programme (UNEP)
PO Box 30552,
Nairobi,
Kenya

UNEP Regional Office for Europe
11 Chemin des Anemones,
PO Box 76, 1219 Chatelaine,
Geneva,
Switzerland

UN Development Programme (UNDP)
1 United Nations Plaza,
New York, NY 10017
USA

UN High Commissioner for Refugees (UNHCR)
Case Postale 2500,
CH–1211 Geneva 2,
Switzerland

World Food Programme (WFP)
Via Cristoforo Colombo 426,
00145 Rome,
Italy

UN Relief and Works Agency for Palestine Refugees in Near East
Vienna International Centre,
PO Box 700,
A–1400 Vienna,
Austria

International Labour Organisation (ILO)
4 Route des Morillons,
CH–1211 Geneva 22,
Switzerland

ILO London Office
Vincent House, Vincent Square,
London, SW1P 2NB

UN Educational Scientific and Cultural Organization (UNESCO)
7 Place de Fontenoy,
75352 Paris,
France

Food and Agriculture Organization of the UN (FAO)
Via Delle Terme di Caracalla,
00100 Rome,
Italy

International Civil Aviation Organization (ICAO)
1000 Sherbrooke Street West,
Montreal,
Quebec, H3A 2R2,
Canada

World Health Organization (WHO)
20 Avenue Appia,
1211 Geneva 27,
Switzerland

Universal Postal Union (UPU)
Weltpoststrasse 4,
Berne,
Switzerland

International Telecommunications Union (ITU)
Place des Nations,
1211 Geneva 20,
Switzerland

World Meteorological Organization (WMO)
Case Postale 2300,
Geneva,
Switzerland

International Maritime Organization (IMO)
4 Albert Embankment,
London, SE1 7SR

International Fund for Agricultural Development (IFAD)
Via del Serafico 107,
00142 Rome,
Italy

World Bank (IBRD, IDA) and International Finance Corporation
1818 H Street NW,
Washington DC 20433,
USA

International Centre for Settlement of Investment Disputes (ICSID)
1818 19th Street NW,
Washington DC 20431,
USA

International Monetary Fund (IMF)
700 19th Street NW,
Washington DC 20431,
USA

World Intellectual Property Organization (WIPO)
34 Chemin des Colombettes,
1211 Geneva 20,
Switzerland

UN Industrial Development Organization (UNIDO)
PO Box 300,
Vienna International Centre,
A–1400 Vienna,
Austria

International Atomic Energy Agency (IAEA)
PO Box 100,
Vienna International Centre,
A–1400 Vienna,
Austria

World Trade Organization (WTO)
Centre William Rappard,
154 rue de Lausanne,
1211 Geneva,
Switzerland

International Court of Justice (ICJ)
Peace Palace,
2517 KJ The Hague,
The Netherlands

5.6 Conclusions

Depending upon the nature of his topic, a researcher should identify the sources of information required for his research. Should a researcher find it necessary to rely heavily upon secondary sources of information, there is little point in pursuing that research.

It is to be emphasised, however, that sometimes the distinction between primary and secondary sources of information may not be clear. Data based on research, in general, is to be regarded as a secondary source of information, but data published by a government department as to its actual and/or projected targets is to be regarded as a primary source of information. The more a researcher relies upon information of a primary nature, the more credibility and validity his research will attain.

---

[1] 24 *International Legal Materials* (1985), vol 24, p1092.

6 Sources of Information – II

6.1 Introduction

This chapter is primarily concerned with identification and utilisation of sources of information of a secondary nature. The limitations imposed by a reliance upon secondary sources should be clearly stated in research. The intention of this chapter is to discuss some of the most popular secondary sources of information and to evaluate their role in research. It must be emphasised that there may be as many secondary sources of information as a researcher can think of in relation to his research.

6.2 Some of the most popular secondary sources of information

Interviewing (a general discussion)

In discussing interviewing as a secondary source of information, the opportunity has been taken to examine the art of interviewing, which a researcher may find useful. According to the *Oxford English Dictionary*, 'interview' means 'A meeting of persons face to face, especially one sought or arranged for the purpose of formal conference on some point.' It also means, 'A meeting between a representative of the press or some one from whom he seeks to obtain statements for publication.'[1] Following this definition, one could therefore say that interviewing involves a face-to-face question-answering session. Such an exercise must satisfy a number of prerequisites. The interviewer must know what to ask and how to formulate his questions (see Chapter 2, p7, Questions et seq). He must also ensure that his behaviour or attitude does not create an adverse environment which would antagonise his subjects. It is essential that he introduces himself to his subjects properly, and indeed he must be well-dressed and groomed. Often, his willingness to learn from his subjects prompts the latter to cooperate and give adequate information. Interviewers must realise that officials are not obliged to give away any information as to their business activities, unless compelled to do so by Law. The onus is largely upon the interviewer to create an atmosphere of understanding and friendliness. Any vanity or pomposity on the part of the interviewer as a researcher will be damaging to his purpose. It must be emphasised that the first appearance of the interviewer plays a significant role for both the interviewer and the interviewee;[2] it can create an instantaneous rapport. However, it may be useful to bear in mind that in most cases interviewees hold the upper hand, generally speaking; the interviewer is really at the mercy of the interviewee for information.

Age and social social status of both interviewer and interviewee seem to have a significant effect on interviews. Interviewers, if more experienced in life and older than their respondents (interviewees), may derive more from the latter. A degree of superior-inferior feeling may develop in an interviewing process. An interviewer should perhaps dress neutrally.[3]

Adherence to different social classes may create a barrier between the interviewer and his respondents. The us/them attitude may prevail between the two parties. Interviewing eminent persons known for their unbiased attitudes on many issues may be a worthwhile exercise. On the other hand, a belief or conviction held by both the interviewer and his respondent(s) in relation to the subject-matter of research may produce biased results.[4] Interviewing is a rather personal matter in that its success largely depends upon the measure of rapport established between the parties.[5]

Interviewing in legal research is certainly necessary in order to find out about the practical application of certain rules of law or international convention rules, or the internal structure of an institution etc, or for the purpose of learning the views of experts in respect of certain legislation. Who should be interviewed can only be decided by the researcher himself according to his needs. Location of subjects on a mass scale may sometimes, however, present a problem. Electoral registers may be of much assistance in obtaining the addresses of people, although they may not provide any indication as to the background and social status of the prospective respondents. Care must be taken to ensure that addresses are not taken surreptitiously and that subjects' privacy is not encroached upon. In the case of a local survey, it would be appropriate to inform the residents (subjects) of the probable date(s) of survey (interview) and of its purpose, sufficiently beforehand.[6]

It is essential that interviewers disclose their true identities and reasons for interviewing their subjects. Research students should preferably carry letters from their institutions in confirmation of the fact that their research topics necessitate their interviewing the chosen subjects. Others must produce some acceptable identification. Interviewees must be satisfied that the interviewer is a genuine person and that he has a genuine purpose. An interviewer may like to explain the reason for his choice of respondents. The primary aim at this stage would be to ensure that no suspicion is aroused in the mind(s) of the respondent(s).[7] If suspicion is aroused, the interviewer may not receive correct answers or cooperation in conducting the interview.

Although, generally, interviewers are more familiar with the complexity of the topic of their research than their respondents, this may not be so in respect of officials holding responsible positions in commercial houses or public, private, non-governmental or international organisations. Therefore, in order to meet either of the situations, an interviewer must be prepared with appropriately articulate and structured questions. It is to be remembered that the patience of respondents should not be strained by asking too many or vague questions.

The order of questions must be maintained. The interviewer should possess the skill of raising incidental and extempore questions, where appropriate. In no circumstances should an interviewer annoy or emotionally hurt his respondents. Where possible, questions regarding the private lives of respondents should be avoided. Questions should be jargon-free, clear and unambiguous, unless a researcher seeks information from say, a stock exchange, where the use of relevant jargon is commonplace. It must be emphasised that, generally, the use of jargon is not necessary to explain anything. In fact, in many cases, questions formulated in jargon or discussions full of jargon may have an off-putting effect on respondents.

Interviews must be as neutral as possible; indeed, interviewers with a certain bias in relation to certain issues or matters should refrain from interviewing others on those issues and matters. As explained in Chapter 1, a researcher should not undertake research on a topic about which he may not be able to achieve an unbiased opinion or treatment. In the event of a respondent giving a wrong answer deliberately or otherwise, a researcher should not attempt to correct the respondent. On the other hand, researchers should not pose questions which are not honest and truthful. Interviews should be seen as cases of social interaction between two persons, the outcome of which may not be free from bias, inconsistencies and inaccuracies.[8]

There do not exist any specific criteria or formulae for interviewing. In fact, unstructured interviews can sometimes produce a more effective outcome than structured interviews.[9] In respect of each interview a special instantaneous environment is created. Nevertheless, certain basic training would appear to be quite helpful in conducting an interview. A researcher must, however, accept the fact that certain information may never be elicited through interviews.

It would be appropriate to make a distinction between a survey interview and an interview for the purpose of seeking information or verifying certain information. Whereas the former is concerned with a large number of people whose background may not be known in detail, the latter is used when specific information is to be obtained from specific institutions, or persons belonging to those institutions, or particular individuals. Although subjects are usually chosen according to certain criteria determined by the researcher himself, survey results are based on generality within the chosen group or section of people.

Command of the language is essential for conducting interviews. Interviewing of an ethnic minority, for example, demands a great skill on the part of a researcher. Even though the language of both parties may be the same, the researcher should be familiar with the expressions he is supposed to use in order not offend his respondents. Extra skills are certainly required for interviewing children.[10]

Advantages and disadvantages of interviewing

Some of the most important advantages of interviewing

First, a researcher can significantly influence the environment of the interview whether it is held in private or in public. Second, the researcher can have control over the order of questions and can repeat a question in different ways until the respondent has actually understood it. Third, the researcher can ensure that all the questions are answered by the respondent and also that the interviewee answers questions personally without being prompted by others. Fourth, the researcher can also study the non-verbal behaviour of the respondent. Fifth, incidental questions may also be asked and answered.

Some of the most important disadvantages of interviewing
First, interviewing can be quite costly. Not only regarding the members of a team, where complex study procedure is involved, but also the respondent(s) may be required to be paid very high fees. Second, there is no guarantee that all the responses will be valid and well-founded. Third, a face-to-face encounter between a researcher and his subjects may make the latter feel threatened/ influenced unless of course the subjects are experienced in such encounters or where subjects may be able to dominate the researcher. Fourth, as the same question may be required to be put in different ways to different respondents, it may be difficult for the researcher to standardise both the questions and their corresponding answers.

6.3 Remote or distant interviewing

Remote or distant interviewing is usually done over the telephone. This method of interviewing can be a successful method of survey research only if a majority of households in the locality concerned possess telephones. The cooperation of respondents is essential to make this method a success. This method of interviewing is practicable only when the information sought may be derived from a brief discussion. There are certain advantages and disadvantages of this method of interviewing.

Some of the most important advantages of remote or distant interviewing

First, respondents can remain relatively anonymous and therefore may be more willing to answer questions than they are at direct interviews. By virtue of not encountering the interviewer face-to-face, respondents will perhaps not feel so nervous in answering questions. Second, this method of interviewing is fast and cost-effective,[11] and therefore proves beneficial to both researcher and respondent. Third, it allows the survey to be conducted over an area other than a geographically clustered area. The sample can be truly representative of the population in a larger area.

Some of the most important disadvantages of remote or distant interviewing

First, respondents may be less motivated to answer questions over the telephone and the interviewer has no power to continue with the interview. Indeed, respondents can terminate discussions at any time they like. Second, such interviews being rather impersonal in nature, it is difficult to assess the effect of the background and the environment of respondents upon their views. Third, respondents can easily decide not to tell the truth, and the interviewer may have no choice but to accept unfounded and untrue answers.[12]

6.4 Mailed questionnaires

General

Standardisation of information based on answers to mailed questionnaires has become a common practice in recent years, especially in survey research relating to business and sociological studies. Questionnaires cannot be correctly drafted until the research design and the subject-matter of the research have been thoroughly worked out. The validity of answers to questionnaires has always been a moot point. They may indicate a trend in the attitudes or behavioural pattern of a section of the population, but they may not be fully relied upon.

Prior to sending questionnaires two points must be considered seriously by a researcher: to whom they should be sent and how much importance is to be ascribed to the answers. As to the first question, the researcher must justify his selection of people, and as to the second, he should not disregard the fact that there exists a good measure of uncertainty as to whether fully answered questionnaires will be returned to him, and even if they are returned, as to the reliability of the answers.

Drafting a questionnaire is one of the most difficult tasks. The degree of response to questionnaires largely depends upon what questions have been asked and how the questionnaire has been prepared. Additionally, in drafting a questionnaire, a researcher should bear in mind whether any respondent might feel embarrassed or offended by any question, whether answers to questions will be based on memory or whether questions impinge on the privacy of respondents.[13] As a researcher cannot know in detail the background of his respondents, questions must be fairly general in nature. Hypothetical, long-winded, complex or open-ended questions should not be asked. Apart from the substantive aspect of a questionnaire, the length, form and the ease of completing and returning it play an important role. Sometimes inducements to reply prove to be effective. Inducements can take various forms: by trying to convince respondents, perhaps in the introduction to the questionnaire, that the study undertaken is very important and that their cooperation would be invaluable; or by securing the 'prior commitment'[14] of respondents by mailing a postcard in advance; or by promising money or reward upon return of the completed questionnaire. This third kind of inducement can cause a problem in that some of the respondents might feel insulted by the little money offered against the time spent on filling out the questionnaire.[15] At least one study reported that inducements such as trading stamps or pencils to fill out the questionnaire proved quite effective.[16]

In sending out questionnaires a number of points should be considered. They are primarily based on one's ability to anticipate reactions of the prospective respondents to a questionnaire – how the introductory letter should be drafted; what kind of postage should be affixed (fast rate or slow rate); whether a deadline should be indicated for the return of the completed questionnaire or not. In the event of a questionnaire being lengthy, it will probably fail to hold the attention of prospective respondents; on the other hand, in the case of its being too short, the purpose of the researcher may not be served.

Although suggestions have been put forward by various authors as to how questions should be drafted,[17] the difficulties involved in drafting the most appropriate questions cannot be over-emphasised. There being a variety of respondents, no question can be called an absolutely accurate or appropriate question. In fact, the propriety or correctness of every questionnaire may be questioned by anybody. Two factors, however, require particular attention in drafting questions: the danger of being too specific or too general,[18] and whether the answers of respondents will be distorted by questions which have not been suitably drafted, or which represent bias.

In preparing a questionnaire, it is not only the drafting acumen of a researcher that matters; the possession of relevant knowledge and information by the prospective respondents also plays an important role in satisfying the purposes of questionnaire surveys. Payne recommended that after a question has been drafted as precisely as possible, one should test each word by raising a few questions – has the intention of the drafter been reflected in the question; is any part of the question ambiguous; could simpler words have been used in drafting the question.[19]

But this is a never-ending exercise. Information acquired on the basis of questionnaires may offer a guideline to a researcher engaged in survey-research, but he must appreciate that the validity of such information, particularly in relation to research in Law, will always be open to question.

Factors affecting mailed questionnaire surveys

Studies have been made on this question.[20] Selltiz et al[21] maintain that the following factors amongst others may affect the return of a satisfactory number of questionnaires: sponsorship; attractiveness; length; nature of accompanying letter; ease of filling out and mailing back the questionnaire; and the nature of the people to whom the questionnaire is addressed.

In the case of research sponsored by a reputable organisation or a government department, respondents may be more inclined to reply to that questionnaire[22] than one sponsored by a relatively unknown organisation or not sponsored at all.

Respondents will find it easier to fill out a printed/typed questionnaire than a handwritten one. Whether postage should be paid by the researcher for the return of the completed questionnaire still appears to be a moot question.

Unduly lengthy questionnaires may not be answered by many of the target respondents. In completing a questionnaire a feeling of 'doing a favour' may be present in the minds of the respondents; consequently, questions should be drafted as courteously as possible. The covering letter should reflect a degree of impersonality. Such letters are usually undated and addressed in the following style(s): 'Dear Sir' or 'Dear Sir/Madam' or 'Dear Occupant'. Handwritten appeals somewhere in the letter might produce a good response.[23] There is no reason why such letters should not be dated.

The setting of multiple choice questions should facilitate completion of questionnaires. The question, however, remains whether answers to such questions can really satisfy a researcher. Although the response to questionnaires by an interested group of people may be high, doubt exists as to whether a researcher may receive sufficient response from the general public. According to Goode and Hatt, mailed questionnaires can be effective only for a highly select group of respondents.[24] The rate of response will to a large extent depend upon how much importance and time respondents accord to a questionnaire. Given the nature of the problems associated with mailed questionnaires, it would seem to be inevitable for a researcher to send out polite reminder letters.[25]

Some of the most important advantages and disadvantages of mailed questionnaires

Advantages

The following are the principal advantages of acquiring information by a mailed questionnaire:

a) less costly than direct interview studies;
b) anonymity of respondents may be maintained;
c) less time-consuming than interview studies, although more time may be required for receiving replies;
d) replies may be easily standardised;
e) no face-to-face encounter between interviewer and his respondents;
f) a questionnaire can be completed according to the convenience of respondents and therefore they are provided with an opportunity to consider the questions seriously before answering them;
g) such questionnaires can reach geographically-distanced respondents without incurring much extra cost; and
h) opinions on socially controversial topics may more readily be obtained through such questionnaires.[26]

Disadvantages

The following are the principal disadvantages of acquiring information by a mailed questionnaire:

a) low response rate;
b) no control over the environment of the respondent;
c) many questions may remain unanswered;
d) complex and yet relevant questions cannot be asked;
e) lack of flexibility in drafting questions;
f) questions being addressed to all respondents generally, individual circumstances are ignored;
g) no control may be exercised over the last date of response; and
h) no interviewer being present, it is not possible to make assessment of, say, respondents' ethnicity or other relevant characteristics.

It must, however, be pointed out that many researchers engaged in business studies and sociological research believe that the questionnaire method is a very important method of information-gathering and that there is no significant difference between the responses of mailed questionnaires and those of the interviewed respondents. Such researchers also maintain that the questionnaire method should be regarded as an initial tool of research.[27]

6.5 Correspondence

The status of correspondence in research is rather complex to determine. Correspondence itself can serve as a primary source if it contains personal and/or confidential information, provided it has not been written under duress or prompting by others. Correspondence between a researcher and his subjects may not necessarily be construed as a primary source of information as subjects are not obliged to convey correct or honest information. However, correspondence between government departments or between governments or between international organisations or institutions of similar status is to be regarded as a primary source of information. Its validity is taken for granted.

6.6 Conclusions

In this chapter some of the most popular methods of acquiring information of a secondary nature have been explained. These methods are primarily used for the purpose of surveys, as opposed to fundamental research. The results of a survey may offer only guidance to a researcher for his fundamental research. Of course, a study may be concerned only with surveys. It must, however, be emphasised that the popularity of survey research (case study methods, in the popular sense of the term) should not allow anybody to disregard the limitations inherent in such a method of study.[28] Information based on surveys is to be regarded as information acquired by secondary means, many of which cannot be verified.

---

[1] *The Oxford English Dictionary*, op cit, vol VIII, p3.

[2] See generally, E Goffman, *The Presentation of Self in Everyday Life*, Garden City, New York, Doubleday-Anchor Books (1959).

[3] University of Michigan, Survey Research Center, *Interviewer's Manual* (1969) p3.

[4] H Hyman, *Interviewing in Social Research*, Chicago, University of Chicago Press (1954).

[5] Ibid, p48.

[6] G Honville, R Jowell and Associates, *Survey Research Practice*, Aldershot, Gower Press (1977), pp90–104.

[7] University of Michigan, Survey Research Center, *Interviewer's Manual* (1969), pp3–2–3–3, has listed a few introductory tasks which, in its opinion, an interviewer should perform.

[8] K D Bailey, op cit, p184.

[9] R L Gordon, *Interviewing: Strategy, Techniques and Tactics*, Homewood, Illinois, Dorsey (1969) pp48–50.

[10] In this respect see B R Buckingham and E W Dolch, *A Combined Word List*, Boston, Ginn (1936); and L J Yarrow, 'Interviewing Children' in *Handbook of Research Methods in Child Development* (Paul H Mussen Ed) New York, Wiley (1960).

[11] See W R Kleeka and A J Tuchfarber, 'Random Digit Dialling: A Comparison to Personal Surveys', 42 *Public Opinion Quarterly* (1978) pp105–114.

[12] See, however, the studies made in the United States by R M Groves and and R L Khan, *Surveys by Telephone: A National Comparison with Personal Interviews*, New York, Academic Press (1979); and L A Jordan, A C Marcus and L G Reeder, 'Response by Styles in Telephone and Household Interviewing: A Field Experiment', 44 *Public Opinion Quarterly* (1980) pp210–222. Both studies suggest that the validity of answers in telephone and face-to-face interviews would be almost identical.

[13] These issues have been discussed in Chapter 1.

[14] See further T Childers and S Skinner, 'Gaining Respondent Cooperation in Mail Surveys through Prior Commitment' 43 *Public Opinion Quarterly* (1979) pp558–617.

[15] P B Wild, *Child Health Care Survey Questionnaire*, Los Angeles, University of California (1973).

[16] C Scott, 'Research on Mail Surveys', 124 *Journal of the Royal Statistical Society* (Series A) (1961) pp143–195.

[17] See for example, B Sudman and N M Bradman, *Response Effects in Surveys: A Review and Synthesis*, Chicago, Aldine (1974); Hoinville, Jowell et al, op cit, Chapter 3; S Payne, *The Art of Asking Questions*, Princeton, NJ, Princeton University Press (1951); and D Cartwright, 'Some Principles of Mass Persuasion', 2 *Human Relations* (1948) p266.

[18] C W Emory, op cit, pp209–210.

[19] S Payne, op cit, p141.

[20] C Scott, op cit; see also W Jones, 'Generalising Mail Survey Inducement Methods: Population Interactions with Anonymity and Sponsorship', 43 *Public Opinion Quarterly* (1979) pp102–111.

[21] C Selltiz, M Jahoda, M Deutsch and S Cork, *Research Methods in Social Relations*, New York, Holt, Rinehart and Winston (1959).

[22] See further C Scott, op cit.

[23] See further G Frazier and K Bird, 'Increasing the Response to a Mailed Questionnaire', 23 *Journal of Marketing* (1958) pp186–187.

[24] W Goode and P Hatt, *Methods in Social Research*, New York, McGraw-Hill (1952).

[25] K D Bailey, op cit, pp170–177.

[26] See further P D Knudsen, H Pope and D P Irish, 'Response Difference to Questions on Sexual Standards: An Interview-Questionnaire Comparison', 31 *Public Opinion Quarterly* (1967) pp290–297.

[27] See further E G McDonagh and A Rosenblum, 'A Comparison of Mailed Questionnaires and Subsequent Structured Interviews', 29 *Public Opinion Quarterly* (1965) pp131–136.

[28] J Lowe, 'Questionnaire-based Business Research: A Note', *Business Graduate Journal* (1987) pp50–52.

7 Techniques of Interpretation of Documents

7.1 Introduction

It is essential for a researcher in Law to know how to interpret statutes or decisions of courts or tribunals, although interpretation of statutes is primarily a function of a judicial institution. He may also be required to analyse or interpret certain reports in connection with his research. Where no interpretation of a statutory provision exists, a researcher may be required to undertake the daunting task of providing one. He must perform this task with extreme caution. Assistance may be sought, particularly from debates in Parliament, previous relevant decisions of courts and tribunals and, in the case of International Conventions, from the relevant *proces-verbal*.

In this chapter an attempt is made to offer a guideline as to how a researcher should proceed in analysing a decision of a court, or an award rendered by a tribunal, or a document where no authentic interpretation of such an item exists.

7.2 Content analysis

Content analysis is a method which is used for analysing systematically the contents of a document. This method is used by many for transforming a non-quantitative document into a quantitative one.[1] On the other hand, it is also regarded as a method whereby the characteristics of the contents may be identified,[2] for example, various types of bias that may have become evident in the contents of a document. It can be a very useful method for analysing the qualitative aspects of a document, especially in research in an inter-disciplinary topic. By an application of this technique, information may be categorised, repetition of same or similar words quantified and thereby the psychology of the author of the document may be identified. Content analysis is mostly used by students doing research in Psychology or Sociology. A number of studies in support of this technique have been published.[3]

The technique is particularly helpful in identifying the various types of bias that a document may contain. Bias can be of various kinds, namely, adjective bias, adverbial bias, contextual bias and photographic bias. Bias may be demonstrated by the use of adjectives in writing a report on the statements made by a person; for example, the 'speaker explained it in his flat and monotonous voice'. Use of such adjectives may create an unfavourable bias in the mind of the reader. It is a case of adverbial bias when adverbs specifically are used to create a favourable or unfavourable impression about the contents of a document. For example, 'the President said sarcastically ...'. Contextual bias may be established in the overall context of a report or document, rather than by referring to any particular statement in it. Photographic bias is self-explanatory.[4]

All these types of bias may commonly be found in articles published in newspapers and magazines. Care should be taken that a researcher is not influenced by such reports. Content analysis is possible in the field of Business Studies, International Relations or Law, if the subject-matter of research has received sufficient coverage in the media.

7.3 An evaluation of content analysis

Lawyers are required to scrutinise legal documents. Familiarity with the technique of content analysis can be very useful for students of Law. This method can easily be applied to examining law reports, in particular, and opinions, including dissenting opinions, of judges, and it may be equally helpful in identifying the political attitudes that may have prompted a government to pass a particular piece of legislation. Content analysis should not be confined to examining only secondary sources of information. It is a relatively inexpensive means of identifying social, judicial, legislative trends and the contemporary social values held by a given society.[5] A researcher should take extra care in carrying out content analysis, particularly of documents of a secondary nature, as existence of bias is almost inevitable in such documents.

7.4 Some guidelines as to how legal documents should be examined

Every document or instrument is a means of attaining an end or purpose. A researcher must comprehend the purpose for which an instrument was drafted. The discussions preceding legislation or a treaty or a convention (*proces-verbal* or *travaux preparatoire*)[6] can be an extremely useful primary source of information. In England, some legislation is preceded by Green Papers and White Papers. An examination of these Papers usually provides very useful background information on the pros and cons of a proposed piece of legislation. Again, in England, debates in the House of Commons and the House of Lords pertaining to legislation under consideration reveal the societal and political implications of it to a considerable degree.

As to the interpretation of legislation, a student of Law should really be able to do this himself. There do, however, exist a few aids. In many cases the national Interpretation Act is referred to for according the correct interpretation to certain words, phrases etc in legislation. Courts being the ultimate interpreters of legislation, judicial decisions containing interpretations of certain provisions of an Act should be examined. In England, the precedent system helps to maintain consistency of judicial interpretations of the Law.

Law dictionaries provide the basic legal meaning(s) of legal terminology. Sometimes it may be useful to consult *The Oxford English Dictionary* for the purpose of knowing the literal meaning(s) of a word. Of course, statutes usually contain a section on interpretation too. In England, two other sources are also useful for the purpose of interpretation and understanding of legislation: *Halsbury's Laws of England* and *Current Law Statutes*.[7]

In many cases, official commentaries on UN Conventions are published. They also contain a vast amount of information and secondary materials. Judgments and Advisory Opinions rendered by the International Court of Justice contain interpretation of certain provisions of various International Conventions. The interpretations of regional treaties, such as the EC/Maastricht Treaty, are also given by the European Court of Justice. Reports of the International Court of Justice and of the European Court of Justice are published and are regarded as public documents.

Each Section or Part of a document usually represents a separate purpose, although they may be inter-related. A researcher should examine the Sections or Parts of a document separately and jointly, where necessary. The printed notes on the margin of a document often include the purposes of its various Sections or Parts.

Sometimes the provisions of a statute may be extended or developed by adding extra Parts to it (see for example, Part IV of the Companies Act 1985). In the case of International Conventions, protocols serve the same purpose. In England, statutory instruments which are, in reality, delegated legislation, should be examined, where relevant.

As to critical appreciation of the *lex lata* – the current law, and *lex ferenda* – what the future law should be – a researcher should examine the separate and dissenting opinions of judges, if any, in a given case. With the International Court of Justice, too, it has become a practice to publish such opinions. Additionally, many non-governmental bodies and pressure groups also publish their views on national legislation or even on International Conventions. It is worth examining these. In order to determine the *lex ferenda*, the researcher should identify the gaps in the current law. In this context, he may refer to published materials, namely books and articles, for guidance.

There cannot be any exclusive formula as to how to interpret a statute or a Convention. A researcher should examine it in accordance with his purposes and requirements too. In the following pages, a general guideline is offered as to how to interpret statutes and International Conventions.

How to examine a statute

In examining a statute, a researcher should look into the following:

a) the reason for enacting that legislation;

b) whether the statute was preceded by a Green Paper or a White Paper (usually the Government ascertains public reaction to the proposed Bill through Green Papers and then on through White Papers on socially controversial issues, prior to its drafting a Bill);

c) the proposals and amendments made at various stages of a Bill;

d) the differences between the Bill-version and the final version of the statute, and the reasons therefor;

e) distinction, if any, between the statute under examination and any former statute on the same or similar subject-matter, and a critical analysis of the distinctions;

f) the preamble to the statute – it often summarises the purposes of an Act clearly; see for example, the Preamble to the Protection of Trading Interests Act 1980, which states:

> 'An Act to provide protection from requirements prohibitions and judgments imposed or given under the laws of countries outside the United Kingdom and affecting the trading or other interests of persons in the United Kingdom.'

The background to this statute should be analysed. Over the years, the English courts developed clear judicial guidelines indicating that an order of a foreign court which would destroy or qualify the statutory rights of an English national who is not subject to its jurisdiction must be regarded as an assertion of extra-territorial jurisdiction which English courts would not recognise.[8] The most important decision that prompted Parliament to enact the 1980 statute was that delivered by the House of Lords in *Rio Tinto Zinc Corporation and Others* v *Westinghouse Electric Corporation et e contra*.[9] This case demonstrates how judicial decisions should be examined and analysed. However, a researcher should examine the progressive development of judicial guidelines to find out whether such development has contributed to enacting legislation;

g) the main headings and sub-headings;

h) ambiguities and weaknesses in the statute, and how they might defeat the purpose of the statute. Often, of course, judicial interpretations of certain words or phrases in a statute may be found in decided cases. A researcher should ensure that he has referred to such interpretations;

i) whether the statutory provisions are too harsh or unfair or too remote from the socio-economic realities. Take, for example, the criticism that the Police and Criminal Evidence Act 1984 provoked in the United Kingdom; again, various opinions expressed in both the Houses of Parliament, academic writings and comments made by action groups should be compared with those rendered by various police-related organisations;

j) whether any statutory instrument related to the statute has been published, and whether it deserves any comment;

k) the initial interpretation of a statute, which is published in the *Current Law Statutes*, and whether any comment on that interpretation may be necessary; a researcher may find the *Current Law Statutes* an extremely useful publication for learning the basics about a statute, but he should supplement that, where necessary, with *Halsbury's Laws of England*, for the purposes of learning what very reliable authorities say about that Law or about the related legislation;

l) where a research is meant to be carried out on a comparative basis, then, of course, the legislative and judicial practice in England should be compared with the corresponding practices in the chosen jurisdiction, but a reference to the legislative and judicial practice in other jurisdictions in relation to the same matter always enriches a research, whether it is to be carried out on a comparative basis or not.

Where however, the thrust of the research is a comparative study of the Law in a chosen area, a researcher must ensure at the initial stage, that he has sufficient knowledge of the relevant foreign language(s) and that sufficient material of a primary nature will be available;

m) in the case of a research on a topic pertaining to domestic Commercial Law, depending upon the nature of the topic, the researcher should refer to the opinions expressed by various commercial action groups, such as the British Branch of the International Chamber of Commerce, the British Bankers' Association, the Confederation of British Industry, the National Consumers' Association, as well as to environmental groups.

For example, in relation to the EC Second Banking Co-ordination Directive, the opinions of the British Bankers' Association and the work of the Department of Trade and Industry (DTI) should be examined. Whereas the former made a critical study of the Directive, the latter, in conformity with its functions, published guidelines as to how the Directive may be implemented at the national level and what amendments to the relevant existing legislation the implementation of the Directive might require.

Statutory instruments

The reasons for issuing statutory instruments have been explained in a subsequent section of this chapter, and the methods of searching and interpreting them are discussed. The researcher's mind should be alert to see whether a section of an Act states that 'regulations may be made under this section' or other similar provisions, and in order to find out whether a statutory instrument has been issued, consult the following:

a) *Halsbury's Statutory Instruments*;

b) *Halsbury's Statutes* for an annotation of the section which suggests that regulations may be made under the section; the Cumulative Supplement and Noter-Up should also be consulted;

c) *Current Law Legislation-Citator*; and

d) *Index to Government Orders*, including its monthly supplement published by HMSO.[10]

Where a number only of a statutory instrument is provided, a researcher should check the chronological list in the first loose-leaf volume of *Halsbury's Statutory Instruments*, and the Monthly Survey Key.

The *Consolidated Index* to *Halsbury's Statutory Instruments* contains an alphabetical index to statutory instruments issued until the end of last year; it is also useful to check the index to the monthly issue of *Current Law*. Since 1974, however, *Halsbury's Laws Annual Abridgements* has been listing, in alphabetical order, each year's statutory instruments.

When a researcher is not certain whether any statutory instrument pertaining to an Act has been issued, the starting point for a search should be the *Consolidated Index* or the *Index to Government Orders*. Always consult the latest edition of these publications. Of course, if a statutory instrument has already been issued in the recent past, a good recent textbook on the subject or *Halsbury's Laws* should refer to that.

The problem of knowing whether a statutory instrument is still in force still remains. A researcher should consult the subject index to the latest monthly publication of *Current Law*. Incidentally, the *Current Law Legislation Citator* only gives the position of a statutory instrument (amended or revoked) for the period between 1947–91. *Halsbury's Statutory Instruments* summarises statutory instruments; however, the publishers of *Halsbury's Statutory Instruments* usually provide the full texts of statutory instruments to its subscribers. Information on statutory instruments may also be obtained from weekly law journals, namely, the *Law Society's Gazette*, the *Solicitors' Journal* or the *New Law Journal*. Secondary sources of information, such as articles published in various law journals, may also provide the relevant information. But, a researcher should satisfy his mind by reading the actual text of the statutory instrument he requires for his research.

Whether a statutory instrument has been implemented by the authorities concerned or whether any court of law has referred to it or whether any judicial decision has been rendered on it are part of the vital pieces of information that a researcher should ascertain; and if the answers are in the affirmative, he should analyse the legal effect of that statutory instrument on the social group(s) or on Law generally. On the other hand, if the answer to any of these questions is in the negative, he should also say so; but, in any event, the intended purposes and effect of a statutory instrument in relation to the topic for research must be analysed.

Techniques of analysing statutory instruments

Common law and statutes are the primary sources of administrative powers, but domestic administration today is largely carried out under statutory powers. The term 'statute law' includes both Acts of Parliament and delegated legislation, and most delegated legislation is made in the form of statutory instruments. Hence, a researcher should know how to examine statutory instruments. In so far as this section is concerned, the purpose is not to write on statutory instruments or delegated legislation, but to offer a researcher guidance as to how statutory instruments may be examined and analysed.

A researcher must realise that an Act may not contain all the provisions encompassing all situations, particularly when the subject matter of the Act is complex. Statutory legislation is often a complementary instrument to the principal Act. The more complex social issues become, the greater is the need for delegated legislation in the form of statutory instruments. A researcher should therefore initially establish the justification or non-justification of a statutory instrument; in most cases he will justify it, and the importance of using statutory instruments to deal with novel circumstances in society cannot be over-emphasised. This issue was clearly identified by the Joint Committee on Statutory Instruments, in 1986, when it stated that statutory instruments have increasingly been used to change policy which could not be envisaged when the Act (the enabling legislation) was passed.[11] A researcher should examine the way(s) a statutory instrument was meant to change the policy envisaged in the enabling legislation, and the reasons therefore.

The issue of sub-delegation and the scope of sub-delegation should be looked into. Without express authority in the enabling legislation, sub-delegation of legislative powers may not be valid – the maxim, *delegatus non potest delegare* is applied, although the parent Act may always override this by expressly authorising sub-delegation.[12] Incidentally, under the European Communities Act 1972, sub-delegation is impermissible except for rules of procedure for courts or tribunals.[13]

Whether a government department failed to notify Parliament in vesting a wide discretion in the minister(s) to vary the rules without making further statutory instruments should also be looked into.[14] In *Customs and Excise Commissions v J H Corbett (Numismatisti) Ltd*,[15] the House of Lords was required to determine the effect of a statutory instrument (Order of 1972) made in pursuance of the Finance Act 1972, which instrument gave concessions to traders by means of what has come to be known as a 'margin scheme'. This scheme was further detailed by Notice No 712. The question arose as to the effect to be given to the concluding words of art 3(5) of that Notice. The crux of the matter was whether it was possible for the Court, under the 1972 Act, to substitute its views for that of the Commissions for Customs and Excise with regard to records and accounts which did not fall within the terms of Notice No 712, but might nevertheless be sufficient for the purposes of the Order.

A researcher should consider whether power was delegated in order to modify a statute, and if so, the extent to which the enabling legislation was modified; that is, whether to broaden or narrow the scope of the legislation or any scheme under it. See, for example, s2(2) of the European Communities Act 1972 and Sch 2 to the Act. Whereas the former provision authorised the making of Orders in Council and ministerial regulations to implement Community obligations of the United Kingdom etc, the latter excluded certain matters from the general power. A researcher should examine why, for example, certain matters were excluded from the general power, and what those matters were. Bradley and Ewing maintain that the intention to use wide language in making the provision of s2(2) of the European Communities Act was to exclude 'the possibility of judicial review on grounds of risks'[16] in the case of instruments made under this section; but they are also doubtful whether this intention has been achieved[17]. Examination of observations such as these, by examples, is important for a researcher.

It is to be considered by a researcher whether delegated legislation (by means of statutory instruments) runs counter to democratic legislation-making, which must pass through consultation, scrutiny and control by Parliament. A researcher's knowledge of delegated legislation in the UK is assumed, in particular the reasons for issuing statutory instruments, and whether a statutory instrument was subject to control, and the circumstances in which a statutory instrument may be amended, or annulled, as well as the impact of s2(2) of the European Communities Act 1972. It is worth examining whether the attention of the Houses of Parliament has been drawn by the Joint Committee on Statutory Instruments as regards the justification for a statutory instrument, including whether it was intra vires or ultra vires and whether the drafting of the statutory instrument appears to be defective, or whether the correct procedure was followed in issuing the instrument. Furthermore, a researcher must find out whether a statutory instrument was actually challenged in the courts, and if so on what grounds; that is, whether the contents of the statutory instrument were ultra vires or whether the correct procedure was followed in making the instrument.[18]

7.5 How to consult law reports

Early English law reports (Pre-1865)

Prior to the publication of the *Law Reports* in 1865, certain individuals took the initiative to publish selected decisions; they were known by the name of the individual compiler and are still collectively referred to as *Nominate Reports*. However, many of these reports have been reprinted in a series now known as the *English Reports*. Reports printed in the *English Reports* also show, at the top of the page, reference to the original report by the individual, for example, *English Reports*, vol 1, *R v Walcott* (1696) at p87. This page number denotes the page number of the *English Reports* in which it has been published. The name of the original reporter is 'Shower', which appears on the top of the page.

The pre-1865 cases are most likely to be found in the *English Reports* but one must note that they are not reported in a chronological fashion. However, they have been reported according to the court structure: House of Lords, Chancery, King's Bench, Exchequer, Common Pleas, Ecclesiastical/Admiralty/Probate and Divorce, Privy Council, Crown cases etc. It is important to identify the volume number of the report, as specific volumes report the cases decided by various courts. It consists of 178 volumes, the last two of which contain the table of cases for the set.

Incidentally, the full name of the series of reports (when indicated by an abbreviated version) may be found in the *Index to Legal Citations and Abbreviations* by Donald Raistrick.[19] Although the Commonwealth, Ireland, the United Kingdom and the United States are the main sources of entry in this work, the index includes entries from other parts of the world too, namely, Africa, Asia, Europe and Latin America.

Of course, the *All England Law Reports* reprints cover cases between 1558 and 1935. This has its own index. The New Series of the *Law Journal Reports* covers the period between 1831 and 1947. In 1865, the Incorporated Council of Law Reporting commenced publishing the *Law Reports*, but a researcher should remember that in view of the complex judicial system originally, there were many series within the *Law Reports*. The style of citation varies, depending upon the year in which the case was reported. However, broadly, the periods may be categorised in the following way: (1865) – (1875); (1876) – (1890); and [1891] – . A researcher is advised to see how cases have been cited in this work. However, he may like to consult Indices and Digests to the Law Reports. The *Law Reports Digests* covers the period from 1865 till 1950. The two other major series are the *All England Law Reports* (1936 –) and the *Weekly Law Reports* (1935 –). Reports on the general cases, that is, those that have been decided by the traditional courts, may be found in the series mentioned above; for others, that is, specialist reports, a researcher should consult the specific reports published for cases decided by special courts, namely, ICR (*Industrial Court Reports*, 1972 – 1974), then, *Industrial Cases Reports* (1975 –). Below is a list of series of law reports that are available at most Law libraries. For foreign law reports, consult each library to ascertain what it has in its archives.

Appellate Series

LRHL	English and Irish Appeals (1866–1875)
LRPC	Privy Council Appeals (1865–1875)
LR Sc & Div	Scotch and Divorce Appeals (1866–1875)
App Cas	Appeal Cases (1875–1890)
AC	Appeal Cases (1891–)

Common Law Series

LRCP	Common Pleas Cases (1865–1875)
LRCCR	Crown Cases Reserved (1865–1875)
LRQB	Queen's Bench Cases (1865–1875)
LR Ex	Exchequer Cases (1865–1875)
CPD	Common Pleas Division (1875–1880)
Ex D	Exchequer Division (1875–1880)
QBD	Queen's Bench Division (1875–1890)
QB or KB	Queen's (Or King's) Bench Division (1891–)

Equity Series

LR Ch or Ch App	Chancery Appeal Cases (1865–1875)
LR Eq	Equity Cases (1866–1875)
Ch D	Chancery Division (1875–1890)
Ch	Chancery Division (1891–)

Other Series

LR A & E	Admiralty and Ecclesiastical Cases (1865–1875)
LR P & D	Probate and Divorce Cases (1865–1875)
PD	Probate Division (1875–1890)
P	Probate Division (1891–1971)
Fam	Family Division (1972–)
LRRPC	Restrictive Practices Cases (1957–1972)

Although legislation may be of two types (primary and secondary) for the purposes of research each type is to be treated as a primary source of information. In the United Kingdom, whereas primary legislation takes the form of statutes or Acts of Parliament, examples of secondary legislation would be delegated legislation, that is, the legislation laid down by bodies authorised by Parliament, namely, bye-laws passed by the local authorities. Statutory instruments, which represent another form of secondary legislation, are regulations made by government departments.

Acts of Parliament are available individually, or in bound volumes (an annual publication), the latter being known as Public General Acts and Resources. After receiving the Royal Assent each Law Act is published by Her Majesty's Stationery Office (HMSO), which is led by the Queen's Printer of Acts of Parliament. Local and Personal Acts which are also published by HMSO each year are listed in the final annual bound volume of Queen's Printer's copies.

Where to find statutes

The two most useful works are *Halsbury's Statutes* and *Current Law Statutes*. Annotations of statutes in both publications are regarded as reliable sources of information; statutes are annotated by experts in the specific field of the Law. Whereas *Current Law Statutes* is annotated and published maintaining a chronology of chapters,[20] *Halsbury's Statutes*, after annotation, is published in alphabetical order of subject headings. In order to keep it up-to-date, an annual *Cumulative Supplement* is also published, in addition to a loose-leaf *Noter-Up* volume (this latter publication includes more recent developments in Law). A researcher may also like to consult Butterworths Direct for online versions of *Halsbury's*.

The principal distinction between these two publications is that whereas *Halsbury's Statutes* is updated as and when necessary, the *Current Law Statutes* is not; this is because the latter is a publication pertaining to the year in which the statutes were enacted. However, it provides a very useful material for researchers, and in addition to providing a basic commentary and history of the legislation, it also makes reference to important cases. Of course, the problem remains that until either of these materials is published, a researcher is required to give his own interpretation to a statute, where necessary. In the meantime, a researcher should also consult articles and comments on a Bill, if any, published by academics and practitioners. The alphabetical index volume to *Halsbury's* provides the year of statutes; a researcher may find this index useful when he is not certain of the year in which a statute was enacted. Another important aspect of *Halsbury's Statutes* is that, if an old statute dating from before 1865 is still in force, it will be found in the series by its subject matter or through the index volume. Incidentally, the original text of an old statute may be found in either *Statutes of the Realm* (between the period 1235 and 1713) published by the Record Commission in the 19th century, or in *Statutes at Large*. The *Current Law Statutes* provides an alphabetical list of statutes published in a particular year. *Current Law Legislation Citator* also provides at the beginning an alphabetical list of statutes published in a particular year.

Halsbury's Laws of England is an extremely reliable primary source of information. Courts also refer to it. It not only annotates statutes, but also provides comprehensive analysis and development of the Law in relation to particular matters. This series is published under various areas of Law, and because the volumes are published in alphabetical order, it is extremely simple to identify the volume in which the particular area of Law has been discussed. *Halsbury's Laws of England* is also updated periodically. A researcher may find it useful to consult all these publications in order to learn the fundamental aspects of a specific area of Law.

Although used by practitioners, there is no reason why a researcher, where necessary, should not refer to *Stone's Justices Manual* (for Magistrates' Court practice) and Civil Procedure Rules and Civil Procedure for County Courts and Higher Courts. They also are to be regarded as primary sources of information. Indeed, in many instances, the judicial development and interpretations of statutes are very cogently identified in these works. A researcher should also be familiar with the judicial practice in a particular field of the Law.

Halsbury's Statutes or *Current Law Statutes* publish all statutes; however, many encyclopaedic text books also publish statutes in a specific field of Law, for example, Planning Law.

There also exist *Current Law Statutes Annotated*, which is part of the *Current Law Service* and *Current Statute Service*, the latter publishing the texts of Acts.

A researcher may find it useful to start with *Halsbury's Statutes* and *Halsbury's Laws of England*; this is not to suggest that other publications are not useful, but the fact remains that *Halsbury's* are the most comprehensive sources of initial information.

Is it in force or still in force?

It is vitally important for a researcher to find out whether an Act is already in force or not; otherwise his research on the statute will be speculative. There are various ways of finding out whether or not a statute is in force. But, first, a researcher should look at the commencement section of the Act, which in the current practice, may be found in the final section of the Act, which gives the short title, the geographical limits of operation, and the date of commencement.

The date of commencement is different from the date of enactment; the latter may be found on the first page of the statute in brackets immediately after the title of the statute/Act; or the legislators may decide to leave it to the government department concerned to bring it in force, hence the importance of knowing whether a statute/Act is in force. In the latter situation, a statute is brought into operation/force by a commencement Order made in a statutory instrument.

Of course, the first source to refer to would be the publication entitled *Is It in Force?* This is an annual volume; it forms part of the *Halsbury's Statutes*, and it refers to Acts of the last 25 years. Acts are listed in alphabetical order within their year. The caution must be entered that the publication *Is It in Force?* confirms whether a statute is in force or not up to the date on which it was published. It is quite likely that it will state that a statute is not in force. Therefore, a researcher is required to look for other sources that will confirm whether a statute has come into force at a later date, for example, the loose-leaf *Noter-Up* volume. The latest monthly part of *Current Law* provides the commencement dates fixed for statutes during a year. But, a researcher must inform his readers whether a statute has come into force on the date of submission of his research. Many weekly journals[21] give the commencement dates; however, HMSO publish a *Daily List*, which a researcher should consult in order to be absolutely certain whether a statute, until the date of submission of his research, has come into force. The list of commencement of statutes in the *Noter-Up* to

Halsbury's Laws is a good alternative to refer to; but this publication only refers to Acts since the early 1960's. *The Daily List* published by HMSO is the most up-to-date source document to confirm whether an Act has come into force or not.

Whether an Act is still in force is also crucially important for a researcher to know while carrying out his research. If an Act is not in force this would mean that it has been repealed or substantially amended.

Halsbury's Statutes, in addition to its annual *Cumulative Supplement* and *Noter-Up*, usually gives the present status of an Act. *Current Law Statutes* and *Current Law Citator* are also good sources of information in this regard. But, the *Chronological Table of the Statutes* published by HMSO provides an extremely comprehensive source of subsequent statutory history for all statutes; it does not, however, include the most recent developments.

Is it in force?

The need to find out whether any particular EU secondary legislation is in force can hardly be over-emphasised. In order to find out whether a particular piece of secondary legislation is in force or not, a researcher may like to consult the *Directory of Community Legislation in Force*, which is published twice a year. Volume 1 of this publication contains an Analytical Register, clarifying the subject matter of a piece of legislation; a chronological index is contained in volume 2.

The English publishers, Butterworths, publishes *European Communities Legislation, Current Status*, in 3 volumes, which is supplemented by up-dates (blue sheets) fortnightly. They also publish *EC Legislation Implementator*; this publication however refers to the Directives issued between the time the UK acceded to the Treaty and thereafter, and confirms the date on which each Directive between the material dates has been implemented by the UK and cites the relevant UK provision. It is also supplemented by blue sheets on a fortnightly basis. *Cronor's Europe* provides information on the business and legal aspects of the single market. In addition, a researcher should consult the publication entitled *Current Status*, and volume 53 of *Halsbury's Laws*.

As to draft legislation, that is, the proposals for new Directives, the Commission's proposals are usually published in their core series and in an individually numbered series known as Com Docs, and often appear on the Commission's website, as well as forming sector 5 of the Celex database. The discussion on these proposals by the European Parliament or the Economic and Social Committee usually appears in the Official Journal of the European Communities C series, also now available on CD-Rom from Context. The final version of a Directive is published in the OJ's L series.

How to keep up with the latest

A researcher must refer to the latest legislation and case law. The primary sources of information that should help him to remain up-to-date would be the weekly issues of law reports, namely, the *Weekly Law Reports* (WLR), or other sources of information; such as the *Solicitors' Journal* or the *Law Society's Gazette*. The in-house papers published by various large firms of solicitors often provide updates of Law and decided cases. Of course, access to these in-house publications is usually allowed to other practitioners or academics who may be on the waiting list for their publications. The caution must be entered however that in the event of a researcher wishing to quote any sentence or part of these in-house papers, permission to do so must be obtained from the firm concerned, and acknowledgement of the source of information must also be made in the research. Of course, a search should be carried out through *LEXIS* and other selected electronic sources.

The other materials to consult would be: the *Current Law Service*, which is published on a monthly basis, and under alphabetical subject headings. The final monthly part contains an index, which obviously provides information on all that is contained in the entire year's publications. The *Current Law Service* Issues list the following information:

a) all the cases reported during a year;
b) all the Acts the provisions of which have been affected;
c) all statutory instruments issued during the year;
d) Parliamentary Bills, and the stage(s) they have reached;
e) commencement dates for Acts to come into force;
f) words and phrases which have received the attention of the courts during a year.

One of the advantages of consulting the *Current Law Service* is that a researcher can have all important information, legislation or otherwise, in the annual volumes, or even in the monthly issues, which is a less time-consuming effort for him. The service is available in electronic form on CD-Rom as *Current Legal Information* and is likely to be fully incorporated over time into the new *Westlaw UK* online service.

The *Current Law Citators*

This publication provides an index of articles in all law journals published in the UK including case notes and discussion of statutes. Again, it is not in itself a primary source of information for research; it is an index service to inform a researcher whether anything has been written on an Act or a case. It is also published as part of the CD-Rom *Current Legal Information* service and as part of the online *Westlaw UK* service.

Other informed sources of a primary nature

There is no harm in introducing students, both undergraduate and graduate, to practice-oriented sources of information of a primary nature. The two highly informed sources of information are: the *Encyclopaedia of Forms and Precedents* which covers all the non-litigious areas; and *Atkin's Court Forms* which covers litigious areas. This latter source is extremely useful in that it not only gives model drafts of Statements of Claim, defences, Notices etc, but also provides good commentary on the existing Law, and references to improved judicial decisions. The volumes are published in alphabetical subject order, cumulative supplements, annual revised indices, and each title is written by a specialist editor. The index to *Atkin's Court Forms* is particularly comprehensive.

In carrying out research, a researcher, as has been pointed out earlier, must refer to the latest development in Law and/or the latest case law on a legal issue. But, he must not totally ignore the case law which has been amended or reversed or the decision in a case which has been overruled by a subsequent decision on another case. It is crucially important for a researcher to provide the reason why an Act has been amended or reversed or a decision has been overruled. This is a process in legal research which may be described as the growth and development of Law in a given area. A practising lawyer must refer to the latest case in a courtroom,[22] but a researcher must distinguish between the old and the new. Take for example, the Arbitration Act 1996. In order to discuss this Act, a researcher is not only required to trace the reasons for enacting this legislation, as well as the reasons for repealing Part I of the Arbitration Act 1950, in addition to examining the special features of the new legislation, but should also bear it in mind that the new legislation may not necessarily disregard the cases which were decided by the English courts with reference to the former legislation.

On the side of case law, take for example, *Anns v Merton LBC*[23] which decision was overruled by *Murphy v Brentwood DC*.[24] It will be imperative for a researcher to examine the reasons why the decision in *Anns v Merton* was overruled. In doing so, a researcher is also required to look into whether any socio-economic reason or public policy reason[25] prompted the court to overrule *Anns v Merton*, and whether the decision in *Murphy* might serve the socio-economic or public policy reason. The same exercise should be carried out to establish why the interpretation of a statute provision in a former case was overruled by the court in a later case; that is, whether the rules of interpretation and the intention of Parliament would be maintained better when the latter interpretation is adopted, and furthermore, whether this latter interpretation has already been adopted by the courts in cases decided subsequent to the case in which the new interpretation was handed down by the court.

In view of the advent of the publications listed above and high technology, a researcher should not usually experience much difficulty in obtaining information on the latest development on English Law and cases decided by the courts, but whereas collection of information is primarily a physical and non-academic activity, which is important in carrying out research, the faculty of developing new ideas on the basis of the information collected is a more fundamental aspect of research.

If a researcher looks for an old or a foreign citation, he may like to refer to *The Digest*. The reader should be reminded however that the most useful index is provided by the citator volumes of the *Current Law Service*, *The Current Law Citator* and by the case index to *Halsbury's Laws*.

The *Current Law Case Citator*
Since 1947, it lists every case, in alphabetical order. Currently, there exist two volumes: 1947–76 and 1977–88; the third volume is in preparation.

Halsbury's Law Case-Index
The origin of this series goes back further than the *Current Law Case Citator*, and covers all important cases.

The Digest
Originally known as the *English and Empire Digest*, it reports cases of the common law jurisdictions, except the US. It also includes European Union and European Human Rights

cases. It is updated by supplements, and its contents are arranged alphabetically under various headings.

The Digest, in its different volumes, will not help a researcher in resolving any research-based problem; it is simply a compendium of case law. A researcher must bear in mind that a subsequent statute can overturn case law. *The Digest* does not provide this information, and from this standpoint, it is somewhat risky to entirely rely on the cases it reports. Cross references of relevant headings are often required to be done in using *The Digest*. It is a good source for foreign and obscure cases. The index does not refer directly to the case, but the title and volume. A researcher is then required to find the particular volume's index as the paragraph number. A *Cumulative Supplement* is published annually; it also has a noter-up section which provides additions and amendments to case digests in the principal volumes.

7.6 Summary

When the title of a case is known to the researcher, he should consult the following.

a) *Current Law Case Citator*, which started in 1947.

b) For cases prior to 1865, a researcher should look in the index to the English Reports. Some series of law reports publish their own indices, eg *All England Reports Indices*.

c) *The Digest* (formerly the *English and Empire Digest*). A researcher should look up the case in the Consolidated Table of Cases, which gives a reference to the subject and volume under which the case is listed. The subject appears in the relevant volume and the Table of Cases shows the page or case number at which the report has been published. Incidentally, *The Digest* has its own User's Guide.

d) For very recent cases, a researcher should check the monthly parts of *Current Law* or the most cumulative index to the *Law Reports* or *All England Law Reports* or the Table of Cases in the latest copy of the *Weekly Law Reports*. *LEXIS* and other electronic information services will also help a researcher in this regard. The researcher should also note that *LEXIS* is a good source for investigating unreported cases. See also section 3.3 in this work.

e) In the case of an abbreviated citation of a law report, a researcher may find it useful to look up the following:
   i) *Legal Citations*;
   ii) *Current Law Case Citator* (Preliminary Pages);
   iii) *The Digest Cumulative Supplement Volume* (Preliminary Pages);
   iv) *Halsbury's Laws of England*, vol 1(1) (Preliminary Pages);
   v) P Thomas & C Cope, *How to Use a Law Library*, 3rd ed, (1996);
   vi) D Raistrick, *Index to Legal Citations and Abbreviations*, op cit.

f) For a lead on the basic cases on a particular topic of English Law, a researcher should look up the following under the appropriate subject heading or look up the subject index of the work:
   i) *Halsbury's Laws of England*;
   ii) *The Digest*;

iii) *Current Law* and *Current Law Yearbook*;

iv) Digests and Indices to series of law reports, eg *Lloyd's Law Reports*;

v) For journal articles on a case, see *Current Law Case Citators* or the case index in the *Legal Journal Index*.

Glanville Williams' *Learning the Law*[26] gives an explanation of the rules by which cases derive their names; a researcher will also find this work useful for other purposes in connection with his research, namely, the technique of interpreting statutes, how to work out problems etc.

g) *Statutes and Statutory Instruments*

Statutes are of three types.

i) *Public General Acts*

These are official copies of statutes (Acts) bound into annual volumes. Each statute contains a chapter number (for example, (C.30)) and the statutes enacted over a year are published in chapter number order.

ii) *Local Acts*

These relate to particular localities, and legislation in relation to such localities are enacted in order to regulate matters pertaining to those localities only. An Index to the Local and Personal Acts 1850–1995 compiled by Rosemary Devine was published in 1996 by HMSO.

iii) *Personal Acts*

These are applicable to certain people and their property (estates) only.

h) *Annotation and Analysis of Statutes*

In order to get a lead on statutory interpretations of the English statutes, a researcher may find the following useful, and they can be referred to as primary sources of information.

i) *Current Law Statutes Annotated*

This series annotates each statute, usually after giving a brief account of the reasons for enacting the statute. Each statute is annotated by an expert with explanation of the meaning of words and phrases, and comparisons with the provisions of a previous statute on the same or similar subject-matter, where relevant. In annotating a statute, references are often made to decided cases. In consulting this series, a researcher should also look up the debates of the House of Commons and/or the House of Lords to study the controversy, if any, in regard to any particular provision in a statute, and enrich his research by referring to them. Often, the minority or dissenting views expressed in the Houses or parliamentary committees prove to be helpful in developing a research or an idea.

ii) Consult *Current Law Series* published by Sweet & Maxwell, which provide the following.

- *Case and Legislative Citators*
- *Weekly Reviews*
- *Monthly Digests*
- *Year Books*
- *Current Law Statutes*
- *European Current Law Digest*

The above mentioned items provide a comprehensive series. Incidentally, the *Current Law Series* provide information as from 1947 but of course the citator lists all statutes of whatever date that have been amended or repeated in the current year. The series that each of these items provides is now briefly described.

The Case and *Legislation Citators* is actually divided into two series: The *Case Citators* and the *Legislation (*formerly *Statute) Citators*. The *Case Citators* gives the full history of any case reported since 1947, including the full citation of the case, alternative citations, the court in which a case has been decided, the yearbook in which a case is digested, and references to periodicals in which the case cited has been considered, and furthermore, whether a case has been in any other case. In order for a researcher to keep himself up-to-date, he should look up the Cumulative Case Citator in the latest *Current Law Monthly Digest* and *Weekly Law Reports*. The *Case Citators* also refer to unreported decisions.

*The Legislation (*formerly *Statute) Citators*

This series is published in cumulative volumes as from 1947. The volumes and legislation are arranged chronologically by reference to year and chapter number. It covers the statutes passed with the date on which they received the Royal Assent, statutes which have been judicially considered and the relevant case, and information on whether any statute has been repealed or amended, and if so, the date. Similar information on statutory instruments is also published in the *Statutory Instrument Citator*, from 1993. The *Legislation Citator* is updated in the loose-leaf series of the *Statutes Annotated* and in the *Monthly Digest*. Information on whether a piece of legislation is in force and whether any statutory instrument has been affected or whether any statutory instrument has enforced any European legislation is provided in the form of tables: a Table of Statutory Instruments Affected, and another table entitled Table of Statutory Instruments Enforcing European Legislation.

The *Weekly Law Reports* and the *Monthly Digest*, as the titles suggest, are updating services. The *Monthly Digest* has a section on the Law of the month for England and Wales, the European Union, Northern Ireland and Scotland. Summaries of cases whether English or European Union are provided under appropriate subject headings. The European Section also includes digests of legislation. Furthermore, a list of Law books published during a month is also contained in the *Monthly Digest*.

Current Law Year Books

Publication of *Current Law Year Books* commenced in 1947. *Year Books* revise and consolidate the *Monthly Digests*, although during the initial period, they were not published annually. The *Year Books* for 1947–51 have been consolidated into one volume.

Although *Year Books* revise and consolidate the *Monthly Digests*, the style in which the *Year Books* is published is different from that of the *Monthly Digests*. *Year Books* have adopted their own style in that they contain Table of Cases with references to the *Year Book* by paragraph number; Table of Statutory Instruments, which is arranged alphabetically; Dates of Commencement of Tables for England and Wales, Northern Ireland, Scotland and the EU, in addition to giving a general index.

Current Law Statutes

This is a very helpful guide to statutes. It gives the historical and legislative account of the legislation, in addition to interpreting the legal implications of each section of an Act, and the relevant case law. In fact, it is a very good primary source of information.

European Current Law Monthly Digest

This series which started in 1992 provides a country-by-country digest of legal developments in both Eastern and Western Europe. It contains a digest of cases from various European institutions, namely, the European Union, the Council of Europe and other institutions in Europe.

Consult *Halsbury's*
- *Halsbury's Laws of England*
- *Halsbury's Statutes*
- *Halsbury's Statutory Instruments*

The Digest
- The Law Reports
- Encyclopaedias
- Law Dictionaries
- Legal Journals

Research in International Law

There is no shortage of primary sources of information on many topics in Public International Law. The primary sources of information in regard to issues of Public International Law are usually the following.
- Treaties, bilateral, multilateral and truly international.
- Resolutions of international institutions and organs of the UN.
- Travaux preparatoires of various conferences and sessions.
- Judgments and Advisory Opinions of the Permanent Court of International Justice, the International Court of Justice, Permanent Court of Arbitration, and of various ad hoc tribunals.

If a research entails consulting documents published by an inter-governmental organisation, namely, the Organisation for European Co-operation and Development (OECD) or a non-governmental organisation, namely, the International Red Cross or the International Chamber of Commerce, then a researcher should obtain them from the institution concerned, unless they are available in various libraries.

The publications in which documents may be found.
- The League of Nations Treaty Series
- The UN Treaty Series
- Consolidated Treaty Series (1648–1920)
- UK Treaty Series (since 1939–)
- US Treaty Series (since 1950–)
      (Incidentally, US Treaty Index, vol 1 includes titles of Treaties since 1776.)
- Annual Digest of Public International Law, vol 1 (1919–1922) originally

published by Butterworths, London. This series became known as *International Law Reports* from 1952.

- American International Law Cases
  (Vol 1 relates to the period 1783–1968.)
- British/International Law Cases (as from 1964/now ceased publication)
- UN Monthly Chronicle
- UN Juridicial Yearbook
- Annual Review of UN Affairs
- Year Book of the UN (since 1947)
- Multilateral Treaties Deposited with the Secretary-General
- Judgments and Advisory Opinions of the Permanent Court of International Justice and the International Court of Justice
- Reports on International Arbitral Awards (RIAA)
- Moore's Digest of International Law
- Word Count Reports by Hudson
- Since 1965 *International Legal Materials* has been reproducing many treaties, whether bilateral, multilateral or truly international, resolutions of various institutions, international, inter-governmental or non-governmental, in addition to reproducing in certain cases judgments and Advisory Opinions of the International Court of Justice.

It must be emphasised however that many countries will have their own collection of treaty series too, and other documents of a primary nature.

Secondary sources of information

Usually textbooks and articles published in various reputable journals are treated as secondary sources of information. However, in so far as the UK is concerned, some of the so-called secondary sources are regarded very highly, and courts and tribunals often refer to them, namely *Oppenheim's Public International Law*, Brownlie's *Public International Law* and the *British Year Book of International Law*. This is not to suggest that publications of a good standard in other countries are not regarded highly by international lawyers. For example, the *American Journal of International Law* and the *International and Comparative Law Quarterly* are regarded as journals of a very high standard, and the articles published in it are often referred to by other authors. There are many other reputable journals in various languages which are regarded as secondary sources of information of a respectable standard.

Researchers in International Law and international relations are however extremely privileged in that they have the opportunity to consult primary sources of information, particularly those that are published by the UN or its specialised agencies.

a) *The Common Law Library*
   The publications under the *Common Law Library* are also instructive and authoritative. Examples of such publications are: *Chitty on Contracts*,[27] *Charlesworth & Percy on Negligence*,[28] *Bowstead & Raymond on Agency*,[29] *Jackson & Powell on Professional Negligence*,[30] and *Phipson on Evidence*.[31]

Incidentally, on English Conflict of Laws and Public International Law, a researcher should consult, initially, *Dicey & Morris on Conflict of Laws*[32] and Oppenheim's *International Law*[33] published in two volumes.

b) *Meanings of Words and Phrases*
A researcher should consult dictionaries, as they are regarded as primary sources of information. Examples of legal dictionaries are: *Jowitt's Dictionary of English Law* by J Burke[34] *Stroud's Judicial Dictionary of Words and Phrases*[35] by J S James, and *Words and Phrases Legally Defined*,[36] John Saunders (Ed).

7.7 The European Union legal documents

There exist a number of European Documentation Centres in the UK; they are, in many cases, only located in various university premises. Certain large solicitors' firms and Barristers' Chambers have a selection of EU documents; however, students may not be allowed access to the libraries of solicitors' firms and Barristers' Chambers. But of course, internet websites provide information on most of the recent documents published by the EU institutions. A researcher may also like to consult the Directory of EEC/EU Information Sources, which may be made available by Law libraries, in addition to referring to *Cronor's Europe* or Vaughan's *Law of the European Communities Service*; and *Common Market Reporter*.

In order to carry out research on EU legislation, a researcher is required to refer to three different types of instruments: primary legislation; secondary legislation and case law. Of course, in addition to these sources of information, the researcher will also be required to refer to other primary sources of information, namely other documents published by the EU institutions, or other institutions in the form of special studies or reports, Judgments of the European Court of Justice, Common Market Law Reports (CML), or the official series 'Reports of Cases before the Court of Justice ...' known as European Court Reports and cited as (ECR) – this latter publication contains decisions of the European Court of Justice and those of the Court of First Instance (see also *Digest of Case Law*).

As to the sources of primary and secondary legislation of the EU, a researcher may find the following information useful.

Consult the following for primary legislation which comprises the various treaties constituting the European Union:

a) the treaties establishing the EEC, ECSC, EURATOM, and the Treaty of the European Union;
b) the *travaux preparatoires* also known as *proces verbaux*;
c) *Bulletin of the European Communities* (for general information);
d) *Halsbury's Statutes*, volumes 50, 51 and 52 and supplement;
e) CCH Common Market Reporter;
f) *Encyclopedia of European Community Law* published by Sweet & Maxwell – B volumes;
g) Judgments of the European Court of Justice.

Incidentally, most of the primary legislation should be in the European Documentation Centres. Most of the Law libraries will have *Halsbury's Statutes*.

Secondary legislation

Secondary legislation consist of Regulations, Directives and Decisions. These are easily identifiable as they bear the number of the year in which they were published, for example, Reg 345/99, but in the case of Directives and Decisions the year of their publication precedes their number; for example Dir 99/345 or Dec 99/345.

All EU secondary legislation, including draft legislation, and recommendations, is published in the *Official Journal* (OJ). This publication has two series: L and C. Whereas the L series publishes legislation, non-legislative documents, Decisions, opinions of the Parliament on various draft documents, the C series contains official announcements. In addition, also consult the *Encyclopedia of European Community Law* – C volumes; and the CCH *Common Market Reporter*, including the loose-leaf collections.

EC case law

The first case was reported in 1954 (1/54). As stated earlier, the *European Court Reports* (ECR) contains the decisions of the European Court of Justice (ECJ or CJEC) and of the Court of First Instance (CFI), also the typescript judgments which appear singly long before the printed version. There also exists the Court's *Proceedings* series, which are published usually three months after a decision has been handed down by the court. The Common Market Law Reports (CMLR) is one of the dependable reports; a researcher may also like to consult the CCH *Common Market Reporter*, and the *European Community Cases* (CEC).

There exist other sources of EC case law – Butterworths' *EC Case Citator*. Then, of course, various academic journals contain discussions of the cases decided by the ECJ, for example: *Common Market Law Review*, *Journal of Common Market Studies*, and *European Law Review*.

Computer databases

Researchers in Law are most likely to use *LEXIS*; it should be part of their training how *LEXIS* accesses EC materials. *LEXIS* has an INTLAW library which under the title ECLAW contains L and C series of the OJ. There exist a large number of on-line databases which have EU materials: Celex, Eurobases, Justis, Nexis, Scad, Sesame, Spearhead (by DTI) etc. EURACOM has CASES and COMDEC files. Whereas CASES contains all the CMLR and ECR reports, since the beginning of these reports, in addition to *European Commercial Cases* and *European Human Rights Reports*, decisions of the European Commission on Competition Law matters are in COMDEC. Incidentally, CMLR and ECR may soon appear on Westlaw UK system.

Celex is EC's official database, and it contains texts of almost all EC legislative, judicial and other related documents, it is widely available on CD-Rom from a range of different publishers.

It must be pointed out however that *LEXIS* and Lawtel may be used for searching references to matters relating to domestic Law too.

7.8 Some guidelines as to how decisions of courts or tribunals should be analysed

There does not exist any absolute technique for analysing a decision of a court or tribunal. In fact, analysis of a judicial decision largely depends upon the purpose for which it is undertaken. Nevertheless, it is possible to offer some guidelines as to how judicial decisions may be analysed and interpreted.

After identification of the precise legal issue(s) with which he is concerned, the researcher should endeavour to find the cases in which such or similar issues have been discussed by the courts and decisions given on them. In England, the finding of similar cases does not present any problem. All standard law reports include a list of cases in which similar issues have been discussed. Of course, computers can be of immense help in this regard.

Where facts are dissimilar but the legal issues are similar, the researcher should point this out, and justify his reasons for relying upon the decisions on those issues in those cases. In every case, the rationale of the decision should be identified and dealt with. In the case of contradictory decisions on similar issues, the judicial reasonings for departing from the system of precedent should clearly be brought out and examined carefully.

In the event of subsequent legislation requiring a court to depart from the system of precedent, the relevance of discussing the previous case(s) should be justified.

The social and economic factors, if any, which may have prompted a court to depart from a decision should be clearly identified. This may occur particularly in cases relating to Family or Tenancy Law. The grounds for applying rules of equity, even in a situation which is to be governed by existing legislation, should be looked into seriously and cautiously.

The key words in the substantive part(s) of a decision should be interpreted and their implications explained. A researcher may often find it useful and indeed interesting to compare similar decisions rendered in other jurisdictions. A comparative study may help demonstrate the degree of soundness of a decision, and hence a researcher may wish to rely upon it in establishing his point.

The dissenting and individual or separate opinions of judges are worth referring to with a view to establishing how the same legal issue(s) in a case could have been alternatively decided. In analysing a decision, it may be revealed that a court felt the inadequacies or gaps in a legislation currently in force. Such revelations give a researcher an added ground or support for criticising a particular legislation, if necessary.

The pleadings of counsel which often appear in the law reports in summary form, may also provide a researcher with new ideas for his research. Of course, decisions of courts often offer interpretations of statutory provisions. In recent years, a number of cases have been concerned with the interpretation of various provisions of the Civil Jurisdiction and Judgments Act 1982.

It may be possible for a researcher to obtain the transcript of an unpublished judgment from the court concerned or from approved transcript providers. With appropriate acknowledgement of the source of information, an analysis of such decisions may be found useful. This technique of analysis may also be applied, mutatis mutandis, to judgments and advisory opinions rendered by the International Court of Justice or the Court of Justice of the European Communities. In the process of his analysis, a researcher may also wish to confirm whether, in his opinion, any bias was shown by a judge or jury in a given case. A researcher should not display any fear or favour in analysing critically a decision of a court.

The following paragraphs illustrate the basic technique by analysing the decision of the House of Lords in *James Miller & Partners Ltd v Whitworth Street (Manchester) Ltd*.[37] There is little point in going into the details of the factual aspects of the case in this context. The House of Lords was required to determine the 'proper Law' of the contract and also the question, which of the two relevant systems of Law, English and Scottish, governed the arbitration. On appeal by the Scottish company, the House of Lords decided that:

> '... not withstanding the important factor that the place of performance of the contract was in Scotland, the selection of the RIBA form of contract showed that the contract was to be governed by English law.'[38]

Although according to the system of precedent, this decision of the House of Lords is binding, unless overruled by the House itself in a subsequent case, a researcher is required to notice that two of their Lordships (Lord Reid and Lord Wilberforce) dissented from the decision. Additionally, three of their Lordships, Lord Hodson, Lord Guest and Viscount Dilhorne, delivered independent opinions. A researcher should examine and analyse each of these opinions with a view to determining the reasons for them and what new ideas could be derived from them. Such an exercise should help him ascertain whether the House delivered an entirely uncontroversial judgment and, if not, in what way the judgment might develop new guidelines.

Two further points also deserve attention in this case. First, whether the place of performance or the form of the contract should be regarded as a decisive factor in determining the proper Law of the contract and, second, the question of combining the two traditional tests – the system of Law by reference to which the contract was made or that with which the transaction has its closest and most real connection. Lord Reid stated that:

> 'It has become common merely to refer to the system of law but I think that the two tests must be combined for all agreed that the place of performance is a relevant and may be the decisive factor, and it is only in a loose sense that the place of performance can be equated to the system of law prevailing there.'[39]

Of course, depending upon his purpose, a researcher may find it necessary to develop other dimensions of the decision and compare and contrast it with similar ones.

The technique of analysing decisions of courts is further explained by reference to the *Re Westinghouse* case.[40] Westinghouse Electric Corporation (Westinghouse) was involved as a defendant in a number of actions in the US District Court for the Eastern District of Virginia in relation to certain contracts to build nuclear power stations. In their defence, Westinghouse alleged that the shortage of uranium and rising prices caused by the activities of an international cartel of uranium producers including two British companies, the Rio

Tinto Zinc Corporation Limited (RTZ) and RTZ Services Limited (RTZ Services), were responsible for their failure to perform the contracts.

On the application of Westinghouse on 21 October 1976, the US District Court issued letters rogatory addressed to the High Court of Justice seeking leave for examination of nine named officers/employees, present or former, of the aforesaid British companies by a US Consular Officer in London so that the information obtained could be used in evidence. The letters also sought the production of certain documents alleged to be in the possession of the two British companies.

On 28 October 1976, a Master made an ex parte order under s2 of the Evidence (Proceedings in Other Jurisdictions) Act 1975, giving effect to the letters rogatory issued by the said US District Court. On 26 May 1977, the Court of Appeal upheld the Master's Order, but ordered that the schedule of documents should be amended by the deletion of certain categories of document. The Court also ruled in favour of the British companies that the penalties provided for by art 15 of Regulation 17 of the General Regulations of the European Economic Community for breach of arts 85 and 86 of the Treaty of Rome constituted a penalty within s14 of the Civil Evidence Act 1968, which would offer the ground for a claim for privilege against the production of documents. The British companies appealed against the first part of the Order and Westinghouse appealed against the latter.

After the decision of the Court of Appeal, individual appellants claimed privilege under the Law of the United States, namely, Fifth Amendment to the Constitution (self-incrimination) and in proceedings under the letters rogatory at the US Embassy in London, the British companies, in pursuance of the judgment of the Court of Appeal dated 26 May 1977, claimed privilege against the production of all but six of the scheduled documents on the ground that their production would tend to expose the English companies to proceedings for the recovery of a penalty (s14 of the Civil Evidence Act 1968). That claim was challenged by Westinghouse but, on 11 July 1977, the Court of Appeal upheld it.

Meanwhile, on 8 June 1977, the Judge of the Virginian Court upheld a claim by the individual witnesses to privilege under the Fifth Amendment to the US Constitution on the ground of self-incrimination. On 15 June 1977, the US Department of Justice requested of the Judge in England the evidence of the witnesses for the purpose of a grand jury investigation, which started in Washington DC in 1976, into possible violation of the US anti-trust laws by members of the alleged uranium cartel, so as to determine whether criminal proceedings should be instituted.

On 18 July 1977, the US Department of Justice applied to the Judge in England for an order to compel testimony under USC sections 6002/3.[41]

By leave of the House of Lords, Westinghouse appealed against the judgment of 11 July 1977. The following were the principal issues before the House of Lords:

a) whether the Master's Order of 28 October 1976, giving effect to the letters rogatory, should have been set aside;

b) whether the RTZ companies could claim privilege against the production of the scheduled documents; and

c) whether the individual appellants could claim privilege against self-incrimination under the US Law.

These issues are now discussed, but first the decision of the House of Lords.

As to (a):

'... the master's order rightly gave effect to the letters rogatory in respect of the production of documents, subject to amendments to confine their operation to areas allowed by English law and further that the order rightly gave effect to them as regarded the witness sought to be examined but subject to the disallowance of certain witnesses.'

As to (b):

'... the companies were entitled to claim privilege against self-incrimination under s14(1) of the Civil Evidence Act 1968 in respect of the documents required to be produced, since production would tend to expose them to fines under arts 85, 189 and 192 of the European Economic Community Treaty, which cover penalties imposed by administrative action and recoverable in England by "proceedings" ... for the recovery of penalty within s14(1).'

As to (c):

'That, in accordance with the ruling of the judge of the Virginian Court, upholding the right of the individual witnesses to claim privilege against self-incrimination under the Fifth Amendment to the US Constitution, they could not, in consequence of s3(1)(b) of the Evidence (Proceedings in Other Jurisdictions) Act 1975 be compelled to give evidence.'

In summary, the decision of the Court of Appeal as to the implementation of letters rogatory was reversed, and its decision upholding the claims of privilege was affirmed.

The *Westinghouse* case may be referred to by a researcher in various contexts: (a) when a letter rogatory issued by a foreign judicial authority may or may not be given effect by the English courts in respect of the production of documents; (b) when an English company is entitled to claim privilege against self-incrimination under s14(1) of the Civil Evidence Act 1968 in respect of the production of documents, where it would expose itself to fines under arts 85, 189 and 192 of the Treaty of Rome; (c) the effect of s3(1)(b) of the Evidence (Proceedings in Other Jurisdictions) Act 1975 on the claim by a foreign court to compel a witness to find evidence; and (d) when the intervention of a foreign judicial authority in this regard must be regarded as an infringement of UK sovereignty.

In considering each of these issues, a researcher is required not only to examine the purposes for which these statutes were enacted but also to refer to the judicial guidelines developed by the English courts, particularly in cases such as *Radio Corporation of America v Rauland Corporation*.[42] A researcher is also required to examine whether the order of a foreign judicial authority is so wide as to countenance 'fishing expeditions' instead of asking for disclosure of specific or specific classes of documents; furthermore, whether access to such documents is forbidden by English Law. This issue should be considered in reference to the statutory provisions such as those prescribed by the Evidence (Proceedings in Other Jurisdictions) Act 1975.

A researcher should also consider whether English companies, such as RTZ, could claim privilege against production of documents required by a foreign judicial authority under s14 of the Civil Evidence Act 1968 in conjunction with s3(1)(b) of the Evidence (Proceedings in Other Jurisdictions) Act 1975, and the European Communities Act 1972.

Then, there is the issue of whether a person has the right in any legal proceedings other than criminal proceedings to refuse to answer any question or produce any document or thing. This should be examined in the light of the provisions of s14(1) of the Civil Evidence Act 1968, and it should be considered whether a foreigner may be compelled to give testimony under 18 USC sections 6002–6003, bearing in mind that:

> '... over a number of years and in a number of cases, the policy of Her Majesty's Government has been against recognition of United States investigatory jurisdiction extraterritoriality against United Kingdom companies.'[43]

A researcher is also required to examine the growth and development of the policy of Her Majesty's Government in this regard by referring to decided cases, a reference to which he should find in the principal case (*Westinghouse*).

Support in favour of or against an argument should be sought from the opinions of judges documented in case reports, as primary sources of information, in addition to secondary sources of information in the form or published articles (referred) in journals. A researcher should find the list of cases referred to by a court in deciding a case extremely helpful, and should consult them to augment his own ideas.

Another important point in the *Westinghouse* case was the policy issue, which became evident in the final part of the decision rendered by the House of Lords. The interaction between judicial considerations and policy issues should be dealt with by a researcher.

A researcher may also like to consider the provisions as regards the taking of evidence abroad under the Convention entitled The Taking of Evidence Abroad in Civil or Commercial Matters 1970, and examine why the Convention provisions were not relied upon when both the United Kingdom and the United States ratified the Convention. Of course, the Convention also contains provisions whereby a requested State may refuse to allow taking of the evidence from its jurisdiction on the ground of public policy or public interest. Depending upon what a researcher plans to achieve, the decision in the *Westinghouse* case may be utilised and examined accordingly. For example, this case can be discussed in relation to the scope of the Civil Evidence Act 1968 (s14) or the scope of the Evidence (Proceedings in Other Jurisdiction) Act 1975 or even the effect of the Treaty of Rome upon issues such as those presented by the *Westinghouse* case, as well as in relation to the limits of extraterritoriality, particularly with reference to the principle of sovereignty.

7.9 How to examine International Conventions

In examining an International Convention, a researcher may find the following guidelines useful.

A study of the *travaux preparatoire* and the discussion of various government delegates or delegates representing inter-governmental and/or non-governmental organisations at various sessions of the UN General Assembly or the relevant Specialised Agency (which are all available at the UN archives or at many university archives). As in examining a domestic statute, the strengths and weaknesses of the Convention should be identified, just as the reasons for adopting a Convention should be determined. Whether any Convention or resolution of the League Assembly or the UN General Assembly has been relied upon by the

Permanent Court of International Justice or any tribunal, and whether any State has implemented the Convention by any enabling legislation (as is the procedure in the UK) or whether it has a direct applicability under the constitution of the State concerned. This issue may be explained by means of two examples. The Vienna Convention on Diplomatic Relations 1961 was, for example, brought into effect by the Government of the United Kingdom by an enabling legislation entitled Diplomatic Privileges Act 1964. But, at the instances of abuse of diplomatic bags and foreign mission premises by certain foreign diplomats and missions, the Government of the United Kingdom considered and reviewed the issue of inviolability of diplomatic bags and diplomatic missions, which resulted in two published reports.[44] Although the proposals of the Government of the United Kingdom did not receive support from the international community in its entirety, it is worth examining these reports to ascertain the rationale for the Foreign Affairs Committee's proposals for the protection of a city like London which accommodates a large number of foreign missions.

Again, in order to be in line with other members of the European Union (at the material time, the European Community), the Government of the United Kingdom was required to implement the European Convention on State Immunity 1972; indeed, this was done by means of an enabling legislation entitled the State Immunity Act 1978. This Act brought to an end the UK practice of allowing absolute immunity to foreign sovereigns or government departments or government-sponsored institutions even in respect of commercial activity. The distinction between *jure imperii* and *jure gestionis* has now become extremely important in the UK practice. But, the need for a change in the UK practice was hinted at by the Court of Appeal in the *Trendtex Trading Corporation* v *Central Bank of Nigeria* case.[45] A researcher should look into the decision of the Court of Appeal, and in particular, the opinion of Lord Denning, to ascertain the rationale for advocating change in the UK practice in this regard, in addition to examining the guidelines offered by the Court as to how to determine whether an activity is a 'commercial activity' or not and/or whether a government department is an alter ego of a State or not. The gaps in the legislation should also be examined. For example, whether the Act has effectively distinguished 'commercial activity' from a 'non-commercial activity'. Of course, in dealing with such issues, a researcher is always required to consult the published works.

The State Immunity Act, however, does not offer any guarantee as to the enforcement of a judgment against a foreign mission if that mission successfully establishes that the funds available within the jurisdiction are meant exclusively for sovereign activities. In this connection, a researcher should refer to the decision of the Court of Appeal in *Alcom Ltd* v *Republic of Colombia (Barclays Bank plc and Another)*.[46]

In so far as the application of International Conventions, the UN Charter provisions and the UN General Assembly resolutions are concerned, a researcher may find it useful, for example, to consult the judgments of the International Court of Justice or the Permanent Court of International Justice or the awards of various ad hoc in international tribunals. In considering, for example, whether the unilateral pronouncement of a State may result in binding international obligations, a researcher may find it useful to examine the judgments of the World Court in the *Eastern Greenland* case,[47] the *Nuclear Tests* cases,[48] and the *Frontier Dispute (Barkuni Faso* v *Mali)* case.[49] He should also look into the rationale on which the judgments were based, in addition to examining the pleadings of the parties to the disputes. Such an exercise should afford him a balanced view and also an understanding of how or whether unilateral pronouncements of States may result in binding international obligations. Of course, in carrying out his research on the judgments of the World Court he will come across many other references made to various published works.

In examining an International Convention, a researcher should consider the norm-making qualities in that Convention by considering how many of the States having legal interest in the subject matter(s) of the Convention have actually ratified it. One should not go by merely the number of States that have ratified it. The *erga omnes* effect of an international Convention must be examined. In this connection, a researcher may also like to consider the *erga omnes* effect of the Nuclear Test Ban Treaty 1963. This point is particularly important when an International Convention is predominantly ratified by either developing States or developed States, but not by the majority of both categories of States having interest in the subject matter(s) of the Convention.[50]

The same method should be followed in considering the legally binding effect of a resolution of the UN General Assembly. See, for example, Resolution entitled the Charter of Economic Rights and Duties of States 1974.[51] The actual votes cast in favour of and against a resolution are also recorded in the relevant UN report.

Often, special studies are made by the International Law Commission on important issues of International Law; a researcher will find them extremely useful – they are comprehensive, resourceful and they must be regarded as primary sources of information. Of course, certain fundamental works on Public International Law, such as those by Hall, Oppenheim and Westlake, should always be consulted.

It is important to emphasise that a researcher should pay attention to the opinions expressed by various intergovernmental and non-governmental organisations, where relevant, on various issues of International Law.

Where national interest becomes a focal point in respect of an International Convention, a researcher should refer to and examine each country's viewpoint, in order to evaluate how national interest may have influenced the drafting of an International Convention. These are available in the proceedings. Take, for example, the UN Convention on the Law of the Sea 1982. A researcher should examine the statements made by various delegates at the various sessions, and the conflicts of interest; otherwise, his research on the Convention will remain incomplete.

7.10 Research on a comparative basis

Where a research is to be carried out on a comparative basis, a researcher should study and discuss the views of the foreign legislative bodies concerned, the judicial decisions, the views of action groups, and compare them with the corresponding legislation, judicial interpretations of statutes and opinions of various action groups in England. Knowledge of the language(s) of the foreign jurisdiction(s) is essential in carrying out research on a comparative basis. A researcher also needs to acquire information from the works published in the foreign jurisdictions concerned. Incidentally, a researcher may find it useful to use specific libraries possessing foreign Law collections.

7.11 Summary

A researcher may find the following points useful in carrying out his research.

a) A research must not present a summary of the existing works; it must offer new ideas based on justification.

b) A legal research must present original ideas, and not be a mere case study.

c) All research must be problem-based, as all research must provide suggestions as to how to resolve the problems that have been identified.

d) A research must be well-planned and proceed according to the chosen methodology; that is, whether based on primary sources of information or secondary sources of information or both, and it should state the objectives clearly at the beginning.

e) Define the concepts; consult legal dictionaries to find the meanings of special words, the meanings of which are very important in the context of the discussion or elaboration of a point.

f) Read primary sources of information first, rather than being influenced by the opinions expressed by various authors.

g) Reasons for enacting a legislation should be identified, and its application by courts should be shown.

h) In order to analyse the growth and development of any judicial guidelines, explain those guidelines in chronological order.

i) In analysing a decision of a court refer to the individual opinions of the judge(s) where available and necessary.

j) Make out chapters according to the ideas you would like to develop in your research.

k) Do not attempt to write an introduction to the research initially, as the theme and objective of the research can only be precisely stated after the research has actually been completed.

l) Do not leave footnotes to be completed later; it may be quite difficult to trace the context or the source at a later date.

m) In examining English legislation, the debates of the House of Commons and/or the House of Lords often provide very useful sources of information and ideas.

n) In examining an International Convention, the *proces-verbal* or discussion, in the UN General Assembly or the relevant specialised agency, will similarly provide a full range of ideas and the nature of debate in respect of the themes of the Convention.

o) The voting structure in relation to a resolution of the UN General Assembly provides interesting ideas.

p) The views of action groups are very important in examining national legislation or International Conventions.

q) Analysis of ideas and concepts should not become over-elaborate.

r) It is inappropriate and even illegal to quote an author's work without seeking the author's opinion, acknowledging the source.

s) Plagiarism or any other unethical act must be avoided in carrying out a research.

7.12 Conclusions

There does not exist any one and absolute technique of interpretation of a legal document or judgment of a court or tribunal. The technique of interpretation of documents or judgments depends very much upon the purpose for which interpretation is undertaken. Words and phrases in the context of a case should be carefully analysed, and a researcher should examine whether the same word or phrase has been interpreted differently in different cases, even though the context remains the same.

In relation to a legal system that adheres strictly to the system of precedent, a researcher should be very careful to see whether a court has departed from it, and if so, why.

Where conflicting legislation exists, it is essential to see how a court has resolved the conflicts, and in the event of no judicial guidance existing, it falls on the researcher to offer some guidelines with justification. A fundamental knowledge of jurisprudence is helpful in the analysis of judicial decisions and in the interpretation of statutes.

Depending upon the nature of the topic for research, a researcher should extend his imagination to determine which of the national organisations, including non-governmental bodies or action groups, in addition to the relevant government, semi-government or local authorities, would be the most useful to approach for information, whether in documentary form or in the form of interviews. A researcher in Law should remember that documentary evidence of a primary nature carries more weight than secondary sources of information, which are usually obtained by means of questionnaires, interviews, experience studies etc.

Validity and reliability of research are the two most important criteria that all legal research should aim to meet. The more a legal research relies upon primary sources of information, rather than secondary sources of information, the greater its contribution to the existing body of knowledge.

---

[1] B Berelson, 'Content Analysis' in the *Handbook of Social Psychology*, G Lindsey (Ed), Cambridge, Mass, Addison-Wesley (1954).

[2] P J Stone, D C Murphy, M S Smith and D M Ogilivie, *The General Inquirer: A Computer Approach to Content Analysis in the Behavioural Sciences,* Cambridge, Mass, MIT Press (1966), p5.

[3] B Berelson and P Salter, 'Majority and Minority Americans: An Analysis of Magazine Fiction', 10 *Public Opinion Quarterly* (1946), pp168–190; F L Molt, 'Trends in Newspaper Content', Annals (1942), pp60–65; and O N Larson, L N Gray and J G Fortis, 'Goals and Goal-achievement Methods in Television Content: Models for Anomie?', 33 *Sociological Inquiry* (1963), pp180–196; M W Klein and N Maloby, 'Newspaper Objectivity in the 1952 Campaign', 31 *Journalism Quarterly* (1954), pp285–296; and A M Lee, *How to Understand Propaganda,* New York, Rinehart (1952).

[4] For a good discussion of various types of bias, see J C Merrill, 'How Time Stereotyped the US Presidents', 42 *Journalism Quarterly* (1965), pp563–570.

[5] See further Walizer and Wienir, op cit, p346.

[6] In the case of the UN Conventions, relevant *proces-verbal* or *travaux preparatoire* should be available at the UN archives. For guidance on treaty interpretation, see E Blix and J H Emerson (Eds), *The Treaty-maker's Handbook,* Dobbs Ferry, Oceana (1973) and I Sinclair, *The Vienna Convention on the Law of Treaties,* Manchester, Manchester University Press (1984).

[7] *Halsbury's Laws of England,* London, Butterworths (always consult the latest edition unless reference to an earlier edition seems essential); and the *Current Law Statutes Annotated,* London, Sweet & Maxwell and Stevens & Sons (according to the date of the relevant statute). For a general guideline as to statutory interpretation, see G Williams, *Learning the Law,* London, Stevens (1982), Chapters 6, 7 and 12; see also M Zander, *The Law-making Process,* 5th edition, London, Butterworths (1999).

[8] See, for example, the decision of the Court in *British Nylon Spinners Ltd v Imperial Chemical Industries Ltd* [1952] 2 All ER 780.

[9] [1978] 2 WLR 81.

[10] Incidentally, commencement and appointed day orders are listed in the loose-leaf volume of *Halsbury's Statutory Instruments,* which is updated by the *Monthly Survey* section; furthermore, as from 1992, the text of commencement orders is included in the *Current Law Statutes* (service file).

[11] HC 31–XXXVII (1985–86) p2; see also AW Bradley and KD Ewing, *Constitutional and Administrative Law,* London, Longman (1997) at p718.

[12] Bradley and Ewing, *Constitutional and Administrative Law,* op cit, at p720.

[13] European Communities Act 1972, s2(2) and Sch 2.

[14] On this point, see Bradley and Ewing, op cit, at p720.

[15] [1981] AC 22.

[16] Bradley and Ewing, op cit, at p721.

[17] op cit, at pp721–722.

[18] A researcher may find *Constitutional and Administrative Law* by Bradley and Ewing very useful on statutory instruments.

[19] London, Bowker-Saur (1993).

[20] A chapter number is allocated to each Act published within a year. So, if an Act is expressed in the following way: The Act 1999 C.20, it would mean that it was the 20th Act perused in 1999. The numbering system was different however prior to 1963.

[21] *New Law Journal, Solicitors' Journal* or *The Law Society's Gazette.*

[22] Depending upon the case in hand, a practising lawyer may be required to distinguish the new case law from the old one.

[23] [1978] AC 728.

[24] [1991] 1 AC 398.

[25] For a good discussion of national interest, see J Frankel, *National Interest,* London, Pall Mall Press Ltd (1970).

[26] London, Stevens (1982).

[27] London, Sweet & Maxwell (1999).

[28] London, Sweet & Maxwell (1997).

[29] London, Sweet & Maxwell (1996).

[30] London, Sweet & Maxwell (1997).

[31] London, Sweet & Maxwell (2000).

[32] London, Sweet & Maxwell (2000).

[33] London, Longmans (1992).

[34] London, Sweet & Maxwell (1977).

[35] London, Sweet & Maxwell (1986).

[36] London, Butterworths (1988).

[37] [1970] AC 583.

[38] Ibid, at p584.

[39] Ibid, at p604. Incidentally, the Contracts (Applicable Law) Act 1990, provides for the law of the country, instead of the system of law, with which a transaction has its closest and most real connection.

[40] [1978] 2 WLR 81.

[41] Such an order is applicable when a witness claims privilege on the ground of self-incrimination but under which no testimony compelled might be used against the witness in a criminal case.

[42] [1956] 1 QB 618.

[43] Per Lord Wilberforce, op cit, at p94.

[44] Foreign Affairs Committee, *The Abuse of Diplomatic Immunities and Privileges* (First Report, Session 1984–85) dated 12 December 1984; and *Diplomatic Immunities and Privileges: Government Report on Review of the Vienna Convention on Diplomatic Relations and Reply to 'The Abuse of Diplomatic Immunities and Privileges',* Miscellaneous No 5 (1985), London, HMSO (1985) Cmnd 9497.

[45] [1977] 1 All ER 881.

[46] [1984] 1 All ER 1.

[47] 1933, PCIJ Ser A/B No 53.

[48] 1974, ICJ Rep 253.
[49] 1986, ICJ Rep 554.
[50] On this issue, a researcher will find very useful the UNITAR study by Oscar Schachter, Mohamed Nawaz and John Fried, *Toward Wider Acceptance of UN Treaties,* New York, Arno Press (1971).
[51] UNGA Res 3281 (XXIX).

8 Layout of Thesis, Footnoting and Bibliography

8.1 Introduction

A good layout is important for two reasons: (a) it evidences the scope of the researcher's ideas; and (b) it illustrates the order of his ideas. There does exist a standardised layout for research pertaining to each discipline, although variations to a certain extent may occur. Variations may be recommended by the institution or university for which a research is prepared.

The method of footnoting may also vary from discipline to discipline. A student of Law should follow the standard method of footnoting prevalent in this discipline.

This chapter is intended to demonstrate how the layout of a thesis should be prepared, footnoting made and bibliography produced.

8.2 Suggestions as to the layout of a dissertation or thesis

The first page

The exact title of the dissertation or thesis which has been registered with the university/college/institution should be typed/printed on this page. At about the middle of the page the candidate should indicate the degree of the university/college/institution for which he is submitting the dissertation or thesis.

For example: Submitted to the University of _____
for the degree of Doctor of Philosophy in Law

After leaving some space, the name of the candidate should be typed/printed, followed by the year in which the work is submitted.

For example: Arnold David Smith
1991

The second page onwards

At the top of the second page the word 'Contents' should appear. The first page of the 'Contents' should show the following:

Acknowledgements	Page
Abstract	Page
Introduction	Page

Thereafter the chapters. For example, Chapter 1: Title of the Chapter.

In fact, ideally, each chapter should begin with an introduction and be closed by a conclusion. At the end of all the chapters there should be a final 'Conclusions' section. This final 'Conclusions' section should be followed by appendices, tables, extra charts, maps etc, depending upon the topic and the arrangement the author has adopted. Charts, maps, tables etc may also be included immediately after the relevant part of the main body of the work.

Incidentally, the manuscript of a book should contain an 'Index' and the pages relating to the 'Index' should also appear under 'Contents'.

The following is a basic structure of a chapter:

Chapter 1:	Title of the Chapter (Underlined)
1.1	Introduction
1.2	Sub-title
	(If there are sub sub-titles the format should be as follows.)
1.2.1	
1.2.2	
1.3	Sub-title
1.4	Sub-title
1.5	Conclusions

The following are the purposes of writing 'abstracts' and 'introductions'.

Acknowledgements

In an acknowledgement, an author usually states under whose supervision he has written his dissertation/thesis. In the case of a work which has not been written under anybody's supervision, the question of making such a statement would not arise. Usually authors convey their gratitude and thanks to those who have encouraged them to write the work and/or given them valuable information/advice. If any financial assistance/grant/scholarship in any form has been received by the researcher/author, appropriate acknowledgement of it should be made. It is only courteous to mention the name of the person who has typed the manuscript and/or in the case of a book, proof-read it, as a gesture of gratitude to them.

Abstract

An abstract should indicate the principal theme of a dissertation/thesis, preferably within 200–300 words.

Introduction

The principal purpose of writing an introduction is to introduce succinctly to the reader the subject-matter of the dissertation/thesis or book. It is advisable to justify the importance of writing the work in the introduction. In fact, it is an art to write an introduction in such a way that the reader develops an interest in the subject-matter and finds it thought-provoking. It is worth mentioning in what respects primary and secondary sources of information have been used in writing the work. The contents of the introduction should be in conformity with the main theme and conclusions of the dissertation/thesis or book. It is for this reason that the introduction to a work should be written last of all, even after writing the final conclusions of the work.

The length of a work should be in accordance with the limit prescribed by the institution or publisher concerned. Pagination should be done in arabic numericals, as should be the numbering of chapters, sections and sub-sections. Manuscripts should ideally be typed in double space, leaving one and half inches margin on the left-hand side and perhaps an inch or three-quarters of an inch on the right-hand side of each page. In the case of a dissertation/thesis, the binding, including the colour of the covers, must be in accordance with the regulations prescribed by the institution concerned.

8.3 On the methodology of social sciences

The methodology in social sciences, ideally, should not be different from physical science methodology. In both domains there is a need for empirical investigation, ie data collection through survey, observation and experimentation. In both fields the beginning of research involves formulation of certain hypothesis. And the research process is the same, ie initial hypothesis – research design – research process – formulation of theories and laws. The differences between the two methodologies consist of the limitations in every stage of research due to the particular object of the latter. As in social sciences we investigate human behaviour, ie subjects that have free will, emotions and spontaneity. The research design based on empiricist method (survey, observation and experimentation) may lead to uncertain conclusions. Therefore the methodology of social sciences must rely more on theoretical development than empirical investigation. This does not negate the significance of empirical method in social science but puts it in proper perspective. As the social scientist is a human being investigating human behaviour he is the object and the subject. This involves a strength as well as a weakness in social investigation. The strength lies in the possibility of self-analysis and the weakness involves the subjectivity of such analysis. The emergence of new methodologies in both social and physical sciences (complexity) as well as the ever-increasing concern for animal rights, ethical and environmental problems is bound to narrow the gap between the methodologies of social and physical sciences. Progress in

71

animal rights issues is bound to limit experimental methods in biology and ethical issues will constrain the extent of social investigation. The rise of complexity paradigm implies the unity of the social and the natural world. Thus it is believed that we are going to witness a convergence between the two methodologies in the next century.

8.4 Method of footnoting

A research student should find out whether his university has published any guideline as to footnoting, and if so, should follow that guideline. Below is a standard method of footnoting.

Footnoting in respect of published books

In writing footnotes a researcher should be extremely careful about punctuation. Footnotes should be written in the following style:

Stage I

(1)	(2)	(3)	(4)	(5)	(6)

A B Smith, *Methods of Research*, Braintree, Hilltop Publishers (1990) p29.

1) Author
2) The title of the book (including sub-title, if any) must be italicised. Each first letter except for the prepositions must be capitalised.
3) The town in which the publisher is located (not the name of the country, unless exceptionally a town under the identical name exists in another country, for example, Cambridge (England) or Cambridge (Massachusetts). Of course, in the case of a US publisher, the name of the publisher will be followed by the word 'Inc', indicating sufficiently that it is a US publisher.
4) The name of the publisher.
5) The page which is referred to or from which a passage or expression has been cited.

All quotations must be enclosed in inverted commas: '   .' The full stop must be followed by the closing inverted commas.

Stage II
If the same page of the cited book is referred to again on the same page of the thesis/dissertation, then the style should be: A B Smith, ibid.

Stage III
If the same author's work is subsequently referred to on another page of the thesis/dissertation, then the style should be:
    A B Smith, op cit, p or, in the case of more than one page, pp.

Stage IV
If the same author's other works are referred to, then in the first instance the full title of the

second work must be shown in the style as at stage I. In making subsequent references, a shorter title of the work would suffice to indicate which title is being referred to.

Footnoting in respect of published articles

Stage I

   (1)   (2)   (3)

A B Smith, 'How to Collect Data: An Example', 19 *Journal of Research*

              (4)   (5)   (6)

Methodology (1990), pp1–29 at p13.

1) Author.
2) The title of the article, including its sub-title, should be enclosed in inverted commas.
3) The title of the journal, including its volume number. The title of the journal must be italicised. Here, a variation is permissible – some authors show the volume number preceding the title of the journal, others show the volume number after the title of the journal.
4) The year of publication. Incidentally, it is also permissible to show the month in which the specific issue of the journal was published.
5) It is important to show the entire length of the article, and then the specific page(s) referred to.

Stages II, III and IV shown in relation to books are equally applicable to references for published articles.

It is advisable not to make references to unpublished works, unless of course, such works are accessible in libraries and public archives.

8.5 Method of preparing a bibliography

The reader's attention is drawn to the bibliography attached to this work.

8.6 Appendices

Often, a researcher is required to attach tables, lists of statutes, cases, treaties or any other documents to his work. Whereas the lists of cases, statutes and abbreviations, if necessary, should ideally be shown at the beginning of a legal work, other lists or documents may be attached to the work in the form of appendices.

8.7 Conclusions

Research teaches a mind to be disciplined. A disciplined mind should set about its activities in a methodical and correct manner. The method of footnoting or preparing a bibliography may seem less important than writing the main body of the research, but pursuance of an incorrect method of footnoting or preparing a bibliography simply denotes carelessness or even a lack of training. It creates a bad impression on the mind of the knowledgeable reader. It is elementary that correct footnoting also helps the reader who wishes to consult the work referred to. Incidentally, footnotes may either be shown at the bottom of each page or at the end of each chapter. The numbering of footnotes for each chapter should be consecutive, and a new numbering system should start for each chapter.

Each section and sub-section should be numbered, as is shown on the Contents pages of this work. Once again, each chapter should start with an 'Introduction' and end with a 'Conclusion'. In this way the organisation of the research is clearly established. All work should end with a final 'Conclusions' section.

Conclusions

There are many methods of research and analysis. Indeed, works published on this subject refer to 'methods' rather than a 'method'. Methods of research in the fields of Science and Technology and Medicine must differ from those in the Social Sciences. Legal Science, which is considered by many to be an integral part of the Social Sciences, warrants a method of research which is somewhat different from those in other branches of Social Science. In this work an attempt is made to identify some of the common elements of research in Law.

It is essential to maintain a distinction between 'surveys' and 'research' proper, that is, research which attempts to discover new ideas and/or establish fundamental norms. Research in Law need not be based solely on surveys, although in many cases secondary sources of information may be required to be used.

In this context, it is opportune to point out the distinction between 'research method' and 'research methodology', which has been very clearly identified by Bailey.[1] Whereas a 'method' stands for the research technique or tools to be used in order to carry out a research, 'research methodology' is concerned with the substantive aspects of a research, such as the basis for laying a hypothesis or the justification for selecting certain types of evidence in research.

A researcher must fully analyse the reasons for choosing his topic for research; he must also be able to identify the purposes of his research. One of his main purposes must be to establish new facts through investigation. Research methods are required for pursuing the investigation process. These methods are not absolute in character. A researcher should not use a method for the sake of using it. What is more important is to raise valid questions to reach the truth of a matter and adopt method(s) accordingly. In order to establish new facts through investigation, it is often necessary for a researcher to examine the growth and development of a matter or phenomenon, hence the usefulness of analysing the historical aspects of a topic. In fact, where necessary, historical development should be examined critically and indeed this process may facilitate the laying of hypotheses.

All research should be problem-based, otherwise, there is little point in investigating a matter. A researcher must not only identify the nature and causes of problems and analyse them but also suggest practicable remedies thereto.

Research on topics of a hybrid character has become very common. In fact, changes in societal attitudes and the emergence of new dimensions of problems due to technological advancement, necessitate such research, which entails knowledge of multiple disciplines and a complex process embracing both survey and non-survey methods of research.

The reliability and validity of findings are the ultimate tests of all research. The onus is on the researcher to establish the reliability and validity of the result(s) of his research. He is also required to justify the method of his research. Combined with these tests is the test of his honesty in pursuing his research. Indeed, if, despite all honest attempts pursued with a valid method of research, a researcher fails to establish anything in an affirmative fashion, that in itself should be regarded as a valid research. In no sense must arbitrariness based on intuition enter into fundamental research.

Fundamental research should reflect original ideas. There is no harm in a researcher putting forward his own ideas first in his research and developing and justifying them step by step, rather than summarising others' opinions, initially. However, a researcher should always refer to others' opinions in support of his own ideas, as he proceeds, as he should also refer to those opinions which contradict his. A mere summarising of already-published works certainly defeats the purpose of doing research.

---

[1] K D Bailey, op cit, p32.

Bibliography

Books

Bailey, K D	*Methods of Social Research*, New York, Free Press (1982).
Blalock, H M (Jr) and Blalock, A B	*Methodology in Social Research*, New York, McGraw-Hill (1968).
Blix, H and Emerson, J H (Eds)	*The Treaty-maker's Handbook*, Dobb's Ferry, Oceana (1973).
Bradley, A W and Ewing, K D	*Constitutional and Administrative Law*, London, Longman (1997).
Bradman, N M and Sudman, S	*Improving Interview Methods and Questionnaire Design*, San Fransisco, Jossey-Bass (1979).
Bright, J R	*Research Development and Technological Innovation*, Homewood, Richard D Irwin (1964).
Burke, J	*Jowitt's Dictionary of English Law*, London, Sweet & Maxwell (1977).
Cannell, C F, Lawson, S A and Hausser, D L	*A Technique for Evaluating Interviewer Performance*, Survey Research Center, Institute for Social Research, University of Michigan, Ann Arbor (1975).
Dillman, D A	*Mail and Telephone Surveys: The Total Design Method*, New York, John Wiley & Sons (1978).
Dominiowski, R	*Research Methods*, Englewood Cliffs, Prentice Hall (1980).
Erdos, P L	*Professional Mail Surveys*, New York, McGraw-Hill (1970).
Emory, C W	*Business Research Methods*, Homewood, Richard D Irwin (1985).
Fowler, F J (Jr)	*Survey Research Methods*, London, Sage (1984).

Frankel, J — *National Interest*, London, Pall Mall Press Ltd (1970).

Goffman, E — *The Presentation of Self in Everyday Life*, Garden City, New York, Doubleday-Anchor Books (1959).

Goode, W and Hatt, P — *Methods in Social Research*, New York, McGraw-Hill (1952).

Gorden, R L — *Interviewing: Strategy, Techniques and Tactics*, Homewood, Dorsey Press (1969).

Groves, R M and Kahn, R L — *Surveys by Telephone: A National Comparison with Personal Interviews*, New York, Academic Press (1979).

Hoinville, G, Jowell, R and Associates — *Survey Research Practice*, Aldershot (Hampshire), Gower Press (1985), Reprint.

Holland, J and Webb, J — *Learning Legal Rules*, London, Blackstone Press (1991).

Holsti, O R — *Content Analysis for the Social Sciences and Humanities*, Cambridge (Mass), Addison-Wesley (1969).

Hyman, H — *Interviewing in Social Research*, Chicago, University of Chicago Press (1954).

Survey Design and Analysis, New York, Free Press (1955).

James, J S — *Stroud's Judicial Dictionary of Words and Phrases*, London, Sweet & Maxwell (1986).

Kahn, L and Cannell, C F — *The Dynamics of Interviewing*, New York, John Wiley & Sons (1957).

Kerlinger, F N — *Foundations of Behavioural Research*, New York, Holt, Rinehart and Winston (1973).

Lee, A M — *How to Understand Propaganda*, New York, Holt, Rinehart and Winston (1952).

Lee, S and Fox, M — *Learning Legal Skills*, London, Blackstone Press (1991).

Lindsey, G (Ed) — *Handbook of Social Psychology*, Cambridge (Mass), Addison-Wesley (1954).

McKie, S	*Legal Research: How to Find and Understand the Law*, London, Cavendish (1993).
Miller, D C	*Handbook of Research Design and Social Measurement*, New York, David McKay (1977).
Mussen, P H (Ed)	*Handbook of Research Methods in Child Development*, New York, John Wiley & Sons (1960).
Payne, S	*The Art of Asking Questions*, Princeton, Princeton University Press (1951).
Phillips, B S	*Social Research: Strategy and Tactics*, New York, Macmillan (1971).
Rastrick, D	*Index to Legal Citations and Abbreviations*, London, Bawker-Sawr (1993).
Reynolds, P D	*Ethical Dilemmas and Social Science Research: An Analysis of Moral Issues Confronting Investigators in Research Using Human Participants*, San Fransisco, Jossey-Bass (1979).
Saunders, J (Ed)	*Words and Phrases Legally Defined*, London, Butterworths (1988).
Selltiz, C, Wrightsman, L and Cook, S W	*Research Methods in Social Relations*, New York, Holt, Rinehart and Winston (1976).
Sinclair, I	*The Vienna Convention on the Law of Treaties*, Manchester, Manchester University Press (1984).
Sjoberg, G (Ed)	*Ethics, Politics and Social Research*, Cambridge (Mass), Schenkman (1967).
Stone, P J, Dunphy, D C, Smith, M S and Ogilivie, D M	*The General Inquiror: A Computer Approach to Content Analysis in the Behavioural Sciences*, Cambridge (Mass) MIT Press (1966).
Sudman, B and Bradman, N M	*Response Effects in Surveys: A Review and Synthesis*, Chicago, Aldine (1974).
University of Michigan	*Interviewer's Manual* (1969).

Walizer, M H and Wienir, P L	*Research Methods and Analysis: Searching for Relationships*, New York, Harper & Row (1978).
Williams, G	*Learning the Law*, London, Stevens (1982).
Yin, R K	*Case Study Research: Design and Methods*, London, Sage (1985).
Zander, M	*The Law-making Process*, London, Butterworths (1994).

Articles

Barton, J A	'Asking the Embarrassing Question', 22 *Public Opinion Quarterly* (1958), p67.
Benney, M, Riesman, D and Star, S	'Age and Sex in the Interview', 62 *American Journal of Sociology* (1956), pp143–152.
Berelson, B and Salter, P	'Majority and Minority Americans: An Analysis of Magazine Fiction', 10 *Public Opinion Quarterly* (1946), pp168–190.
Cartwright, D	'Some Principles of Mass Persuasion', 2 *Human Relations* (1948), p266.
Childers, T and Skinner, S	'Gaining Respondent Cooperation in Mail Surveys through Prior Commitment', 43 *Public Opinion Quarterly* (1979), pp558–561.
Frazier, G and Bird, K	'Increasing the Response to a Mail Questionnaire', 23 *Journal of Marketing* (1958), pp186–197.
Galliher, F	'The Protection of Human Subjects: A Re-examination of the Professional Code of Ethics', *The American Sociologists* (1973), pp93–100.
Heberlein, T A and Baumgartner, R	'Factors Affecting Response Rates to Mailed Questionnaires', 43 *American Sociological Review* (1978), pp447–462.
Jones, W	'Generalising Mail Survey Inducement Methods: Population Interactions with Anonymity and Sponsorship', 43 *Public Opinion Quarterly* (1979), pp102–111.

Jordan, L A, Marcus, A C and Reeder, L G — 'Response Styles in Telephone and Household Interviewing: A Field Experiment', 44 *Public Opinion Quarterly* (1980), pp210–222.

Kelman, H C — 'Human Use of Human Subjects: The Problem of Deception in Social Psychological Experiments', 67 *Psychological Bulletin* (1967), pp1–11.

Kleeka, W R and Tuchfarber, A J — 'Random Digit Dialling: A Comparison to Personal Surveys', 42 *Public Opinion Quarterly* (1978), pp105–114.

Klein, M W and Maloby, N — 'Newspaper Objectivity in the 1952 Campaign', 31 *Journalism Quarterly* (1954), pp285–296.

Knudsen, P D, Pope, H and Irish, D P — 'Response Difference to Questions on Sexual Standards: An Interview Questionnaire Comparison', 31 *Public Opinion Quarterly* (1967), pp290–297.

Larson, O N, Gray, L N and Fortis, J G — 'Goals and Goal-achievement Methods in Television Contest: Models for Anomie', 33 *Sociological Inquiry* (1963), pp180–196.

Lowe, J — 'Questionnaire-based Business Research: A Note', *Business Graduate Journal* (1987), pp50–52.

McDonagh, E G and Rosenblum, A — 'A Comparison of Mailed Questionnaires and Subsequent Structured Interviews', 29 *Public Opinion Quarterly* (1965), pp131–136.

Merrill, J C — 'How Time Stereotyped Three US Presidents', 42 *Journalism Quarterly* (1965), pp563–570.

Mott, F L — 'Trends in Newspaper Content', *Annals* (1942), pp60–65.

Rocher, G A — 'Effective Techniques in Increasing Response to Mailed Questionnaires', 27 *Public Opinion Quarterly* (1963), pp299–302.

Schuman, H and Prosser, S   'The Open and Closed Question', 44
                             American Sociological Review (1979),
                             pp692–712.

Scott, A J   'Monetary Incentives in Mail Surveys', 39
                             Public Opinion Quarterly (1975),
                             pp111–116.

Scott, C   'Research on Mail Surveys', 124 *Journal of
                             the Royal Statistical Society* (Series A
                             (1961), pp143–195.

Thorne, B   'You Still Takin' Notes? Fieldwork and
                             Problems of Informed Consent', 27 *Social
                             Problems* (1980), pp284–297.

Wallace, D   'A Case for and against Mailed
                             Questionnaires', 18 *Public Opinion
                             Quarterly* (1954), pp40–52.

Index

Cracknell's Companions

Cases & Statutes

A comprehensive and informative law student's encyclopaedia, specific to each particular topic. *Cracknell's Companions* include all relevant statutory material (in its updated form) for each subject area, and a wealth of case notes, summaries and comment on all relevant caselaw with which the law student must be familiar. Now re-vamped for the millenium, in an eye-catching, user-friendly new format, makes it an essential aid to mastering the key elements of any law subject.

Constitutional Law
5th edition
ISBN 1 85836 298 9
Soft cover 246 x 175 mm
440 pages   £11.95
Published 2000

English Legal System
5th edition
ISBN 1 85836 059 5
Soft cover 246 x 175 mm
330 pages approx   £11.95
Due January 2001

Contract Law
11th edition
ISBN 1 85836 275 X
Soft cover 246 x 175 mm
376 pages   £11.95
Published 2000

Torts
9th edition
ISBN 1 85836 060 9
Soft cover 246 x 175 mm
360 pages   £11.95
Published 2000

Criminal Law
6th edition
ISBN 1 85836 300 4
Soft cover 246 x 175 mm
456 pages   £11.95
Published 2000

For further information on contents or to place an order, please contact:
Mail Order
Old Bailey Press
200 Greyhound Road
London
W14 9RY

Telephone No: 020 7385 3377
Fax No: 020 7381 3377

1998–1999 Suggested Solutions

The Suggested Solutions series provides examples of full answers to the questions regularly set by examiners. Each suggested solution has been broken down into three stages: general comment, skeleton solution and suggested solution. This format clearly enables the student to see the precise approach taken by the writer in answering each type of question set. The examination questions included within the text are all past examination questions set by the London University. The full opinion answers will undoubtedly assist you with your research and further your understanding and appreciation of the subject in question.

All texts in the series are priced at £6.95 and are written by experienced academic lawyers.

Publication date February 2001.

Constitutional Law
ISBN: 1 85836 389 6

Jurisprudence and Legal Theory
ISBN: 1 85836 393 4

Contract Law
ISBN: 1 85836 390 X

Land Law
ISBN: 1 85836 394 2

Criminal Law
ISBN: 1 85836 391 8

Law of Tort
ISBN: 1 85836 395 0

English Legal System
ISBN: 1 85836 392 6

Law of Trusts
ISBN: 1 85836 396 9

For further information on contents or to place
an order, please contact:
Mail Order
Old Bailey Press
200 Greyhound Road
London
W14 9RY

Telephone No: 020 7385 3377
Fax No: 020 7381 3377

Old Bailey Press

The Old Bailey Press integrated student law library is tailor-made to help you at every stage of your studies from the preliminaries of each subject through to the final examination. The series of Textbooks, Revision WorkBooks, 150 Leading Cases/Casebooks and Cracknell's Statutes are interrelated to provide you with a comprehensive set of study materials.

You can buy Old Bailey Press books from your University Bookshop, your local Bookshop, direct using this form, or you can order a free catalogue of our titles from the address shown overleaf.

The following subjects each have a Textbook, 150 Leading Cases/Casebook, Revision WorkBook and Cracknell's Statutes unless otherwise stated.

Administrative Law
Commercial Law
Company Law
Conflict of Laws
Constitutional Law
Conveyancing (Textbook and Casebook)
Criminal Law
Criminology (Textbook and Sourcebook)
English and European Legal Systems
Equity and Trusts
Evidence
Family Law
Jurisprudence: The Philosophy of Law (Textbook, Sourcebook and
    Revision WorkBook)
Land: The Law of Real Property
Law of International Trade
Law of the European Union
Legal Skills and System
Obligations: Contract Law
Obligations: The Law of Tort
Public International Law
Revenue Law (Textbook,
    Sourcebook and Revision
    WorkBook)
Succession

Mail order prices:	
Textbook	£11.95
150 Leading Cases/Casebook	£9.95
Revision WorkBook	£7.95
Cracknell's Statutes	£9.95
Suggested Solutions 1998–1999	£6.95
Law Update 2000	£9.95
The Practitioner's Handbook 2000	£54.95

To complete your order, please fill in the form below:

Module	Books required	Quantity	Price	Cost
		Postage		
		TOTAL		

For Europe, add 15% postage and packing (£20 maximum).
For the rest of the world, add 40% for airmail.

ORDERING

By telephone to Mail Order at 020 7385 3377, with your credit card to hand.

By fax to 020 7381 3377 (giving your credit card details).

By post to:

Mail Order, Old Bailey Press, 200 Greyhound Road, London W14 9RY.

When ordering by post, please enclose full payment by cheque or banker's draft, or complete the credit card details below. You may also order a free catalogue of our complete range of titles from this address.

We aim to despatch your books within 3 working days of receiving your order.

Name

Address

Postcode   Telephone

Total value of order, including postage: £

I enclose a cheque/banker's draft for the above sum, or

charge my   ☐ Access/Mastercard   ☐ Visa   ☐ American Express
Card number

☐☐☐☐ ☐☐☐☐ ☐☐☐☐ ☐☐☐☐

Expiry date   ☐☐☐☐

Signature: ....Date: ....